Look Out

A Selection of Writings

Other Books by Gary Snyder

THE BACK COUNTRY*

EARTH HOUSE HOLD*

MOUNTAINS AND RIVERS WITHOUT END

MYTHS AND TEXTS*

NO NATURE: NEW AND SELECTED POEMS

A PLACE IN SPACE

THE PRACTICE OF THE WILD

THE REAL WORK: INTERVIEWS AND TALKS,
1964–1979*

REGARDING WAVE*

TURTLE ISLAND*

available from New Directions

Gary Snyder

Look Out
A Selection of Writings

A NEW DIRECTIONS
PAPERBOOK

Manufactured in the United States of America
First published as a New Directions Bibelot in 2002
Published simultaneously in Canada by Penguin Books Canada Limited
New Directions Books are printed on acid-free paper.
ISBN-13: 978-0-8112-1525-3

"What to Tell, Still" originally appeared in *Sulfur*. The epigraph, "Poem Left in Sourdough Mountain Lookout," originally appeared in *Left Out in the Rain: New Poems 1947–1985*, published by North Point Press; copyright © 1986 by Gary Snyder, reprinted here by arrangement with Farrar, Straus & Giroux, Inc.

Library of Congress Cataloging-in-Publication Data

Snyder, Gary, 1930–
Look out: a selection of writings / Gary Snyder.
p. cm.
ISBN 0-8112-1525-3 (alk. paper)
1. Snyder, Gary, 1930– Interviews. 2. Poets, American—20th century—Interviews.
I. Title.
PS3569.N88 A6 2002
811'.54—dc21   2002007493

10 9 8 7 6 5 4 3

New Directions Books are published for James Laughlin
by New Directions Publishing Corporation,
80 Eighth Avenue, New York 10011

Dedicated to James Laughlin

Poem Left in Sourdough Mountain Lookout

I the poet Gary Snyder
Stayed six weeks in fifty-three
On this ridge and on this rock
& saw what every Lookout sees,
Saw these mountains shift about
& end up on the ocean floor
Saw the wind and waters break
The branchéd deer, the Eagle's eye,
& when pray tell, shall Lookouts die?

Contents

Remembering J. Laughlin

I first heard the name of James Laughlin while a student in Oregon. I had been reading Ezra Pound's *Selected Letters*. I had been drawn to Pound via my interest in East Asian art and went from there to Pound's poetry. Then I discovered what Eliot Weinberger calls "the list" and it was New Directions that brought me to the rest of twentieth-century modernist writing. Edward Dahlberg, Rimbaud, Gertrude Stein, Paul Goodman, Djuna Barnes, William Carlos Williams—and so many others—were the writers whose wake we sailed in.

Later, as a graduate student in East Asian languages at Berkeley and meeting the artists and poets of the Bay Area, I learned more of J. through Kenneth Rexroth. Rexroth—it turned out—knew Laughlin quite well; they skied and sometimes climbed together. New Directions was Kenneth's main publisher.

Kenneth always had terrible things to say about Ezra Pound, not just his politics but his poetics. Pound—Rexroth—two very different men. But J. was friend, publisher, and colleague to both and clearly liked them each for their own special qualities. I became aware of Laughlin's "mahayana" or "big open spirit" in this way.

I think it was Don Allen who connected me with J. They were all at a party in San Francisco one of those years in the early '60s when I was living in Japan. A friend wrote me to say that over drinks, Don (of Gray Fox Press) had said to J., "Why don't you take a good look at the work of Gary Snyder." And supposedly James had replied, "those Beat Generation guys never answer their mail." At any rate, one day in Kyoto I received a note from James Laughlin of New Directions asking, "Would you show me some poems?"

I sent him the manuscript of *The Back Country*—and J. accepted it. By the time we had completed the transaction (and the book was published) he wrote to say, "I am so glad you are a person that promptly answers his mail."

That was the beginning of a long association. I finally met him while on a brief trip to the United States and was graciously taken to lunch, met the whole remarkable staff, and entered into a productive friendship—in which I remained properly awed by the honor of being with such an eminent press and under the wing of such a great and sophisticated literary man.

I returned from East Asia to live on the West Coast in 1969. A few more trips around the country, hanging out in New York City, and hearing horror tales of publishers from other writers, and I came to realize indeed how lucky I was to be with Laughlin; the steadiness, the integrity, the respect for writers was a culture that pervaded the entire office.

J. kept up his end of our correspondence (as he did with so many)—it was an intelligent, quirky, friendly unpretentious exchange. One time I felt moved to write him and tell him how grateful I was that his press was there for me to work with. Later I left New Directions to be with a publisher based on the West Coast and nearer to my immediate interests of that time, and also because I had (mistakenly I realize now) thought I had read into an interview that J. once gave about what would happen after he died, an instruction to begin to look for another publisher to handle my work. He was hurt I think, something I had not wished—but that was soon past and we remained friends and fellow-poets.

We also shared an interest in the cultures of India and East Asia. Though my knowledge of Mediterranean culture and the classics was scanty, Laughlin's poetic engagement with classic references and themes fascinated and instructed me.

I only saw J. occasionally; I was not an intimate in any sense; but I knew that here was a man of strength, accomplishment and learning. James Laughlin was a man who while furthering the careers of many others, tended to keep himself in hiding, and then in the end turned out to be as good as any of us.

I saw J. at work a few times—once when I was staying as a guest in the Bank Street apartment and he came in as I was leaving, so that we overlapped half a day. He was dictating a letter into a little tape recorder even as we chatted. I never wrote a letter to J. that he didn't answer. Looking back I realize that the letter-writing spirit belongs to the "old days," an "old days" which I am now part of too, a time when people took pleasure in writing letters—often by hand—and were gratified, truly, to find others who would be timely and generous in sharing their thoughts and feelings in this medium. But grace and appropriate etiquette, good form and good playfulness, conviviality and integrity, are timeless. J. Laughlin's cool, elegant, understated wit and his alertness came out of Poet's mind, wild mind. J. was a fine skier and I would like to claim him as an urbane mountain man.

6.I.98 Gary Snyder

Look Out

A Selection of Writings

from
The Back Country (1968)

Fire in the Hole

Squatting a day in the sun,
    one hand turning the steeldrill,
one, swinging the four pound singlejack hammer
                       down.
three inches an hour
granite bullhump boulder
             square in the trail.
above, the cliffs,
            of Piute Mountain waver.
sweat trickles down my back.

why does this day keep coming into mind.
a job in the rock hills
    aching arms
             the muletracks
                   arching blinding sky,
    noon sleep under
            snake-scale juniper limbs.

that the mind
    entered the tip of steel.
the arm fell
    like breath.
the valley, reeling,
           on the pivot of that drill—
twelve inches deep we packed the charge
    dynamite on mules

                              like frankincense.

Fire in the hole!
Fire in the hole!
Fire in the hole!

jammed the plunger down.
thru dust
                              and sprinkling stone
strolld back to see:
hands and arms and shoulders
free.

Foxtail Pine

bark smells like pineapple: Jeffries
cones prick your hand: Ponderosa

nobody knows what they are, saying
"needles three to a bunch."

        turpentine tin can hangers
        high lead riggers

"the true fir cone stands straight,
the doug fir cone hangs down."

—wild pigs eat acorns in those hills
cascara cutters
tanbark oak bark gatherers
myrtlewood burl bowl-makers
little cedar dolls,
        baby girl born from the split crotch

                    of a plum
               daughter of the moon—

foxtail pine with a
clipped curve-back cluster of tight
          five-needle bunches
     the rough red bark scale
and jigsaw pieces sloughed off
               scattered on the ground.
—what am I doing saying "foxtail pine"?

these conifers whose home was ice
age tundra, taiga, they of the
          naked sperm
do whitebark pine and white pine seem the same?

     a sort of tree
     its leaves are needles
     like a fox's brush
(I call him fox because he looks that way)
     and call this other thing, a
          foxtail pine.

Hitch Haiku

They didn't hire him
               so he ate his lunch alone:
the noon whistle

          •   •   •

Cats shut down
                    deer thread through
men all eating lunch

    •   •   •

Frying hotcakes in a dripping shelter
                    Fu Manchu
Queets Indian Reservation in the rain

    •   •   •

A truck went by
                    three hours ago:
Smoke Creek desert

    •   •   •

Jackrabbit eyes all night
   breakfast in Elko.

    •   •   •

Old kanji hid by dirt
on skidroad Jap town walls
                    down the hill
to the Wobbly hall

Seattle

Spray drips from the cargo-booms
a fresh-chipped winch
                    spotted with red lead
young fir—
                    soaking in summer rain

8

•   •   •

Over the Mindanao Deep

Scrap brass
            dumpt off the fantail
falling six miles

•   •   •

[*The following two were written on classical
themes while traveling through Sappho, Washington.
The first is by Thomas L. Hoodlatch.*]

Moonlight on the burned-out temple—
            wooden horse shit.

Sunday dinner in Ithaca—
            the twang of a bowstring

•   •   •

After weeks of watching the roof leak
            I fixed it tonight
by moving a single board

•   •   •

*A freezing morning in October in the high
Sierra crossing Five Lakes Basin to the
Kaweahs with Bob Greensfelder and Claude Dalenburg*

Stray white mare
            neck rope dangling
forty miles from farms.

•   •   •

9

Back from the Kaweahs

Sundown, Timber Gap
      —sat down—
          dark firs.
  dirty;   cold;
too tired to talk

•   •   •

Cherry blossoms at Hood river
        rusty sand near Tucson
mudflats of Willapa Bay

•   •   •

Pronghorn country

Steering into the sun
        glittering jewel-road
shattered obsidian

•   •   •

The mountain walks over the water!
Rain down from the mountain!
        high bleat of a
cow elk
    over blackberries

•   •   •

A great freight truck
        lit like a town
through the dark stony desert

•   •   •

Drinking hot saké
                toasting fish on coals
    the motorcycle
out   parked in the rain.

•   •   •

Switchback

turn, turn,
and again,   hard-
scrabble
steep travel a-
head.

The Manichaeans

for Joanne

Our portion of fire
        at this end of the milky way
(the Tun-huang fragments say, Eternal Light)
Two million years from M 31
        the galaxy in Andromeda—
My eyes sting with these relics.
Fingers mark time.
        semen is everywhere
Two million seeds in a spurt.

Bringing hand close to your belly
        a shade off touching,
Until it feels the radiating warmth.

Your far off laughter
Is an earthquake in your thigh.
Coild like Ourabouros
    we are the Naga King
This bed is Eternal Chaos
        —and wake in a stream of light.

Cable-car cables
Whip over their greast rollers
Two feet underground.
    hemmed in by mysteries
    all moving in order.
A moment at this wide intersection,
Stoplights change, they are
    catastrophes among stars,
A red whorl of minotaurs
        gone out.
The trumpet of doom
    from a steamship at Pier 41.

Your room is cold,
    in the shade-drawn dusk inside
Light the oven, leave it open
Semi transparent jet flames rise
        fire,
Together we make eight pounds of
Pure white mineral ash.

Your body is fossil
As you rest with your chin back
  —your arms are still flippers
      your lidded eyes lift from a swamp
Let us touch—for if two lie together
Then they have warmth.

We shall sink in this heat
                of our arms
Blankets like rock-strata fold
                dreaming as
                Shiva and Shakti
And keep back the cold.

The Six Hells of the Engine Room

The Hot Air Hell of the fiddley where rails
are too hot to touch and your shoes burn

The oily cramp Hell of the bilges
painting underside pipes—saltwater and oil
ankledeep slosh in the shoe.

Inside-the-boiler Hell, you go in through a
hot brick hole where it's black
and radiates heat

Back of the boilers-Hell soogying valve-wheels
                and flanges

Shaft Alley Hell getting rubbed by the rough
spinning shaft

Paint Locker Hell, it smells fumes,
your hands get all sticky.

Mother of the Buddhas, Queen of Heaven, Mother of the Sun; Marici, Goddess of the Dawn

for Bhikku Ghosananda

old sow in the mud
bristles caked black
down her powerful neck

tiny hooves churn
squat body slithering
deep in food dirt

her warm filth,
deep-plowing snout,
dragging teats

those who keep her
or eat her
are cast out

she turns her small eye
from earth to
look up at me.

Nalanda, Bihar

To the Chinese Comrades

The armies of China and Russia
Stand facing across a wide plain.
Krushchev on one side and Mao on the other,
Krushchev calls out
    "Pay me the money you owe me!"
Mao laughs and laughs. long hair flops.
His face round and smooth.
The armies start marching—they meet—
Without clashing, they march through each other,
Lines between lines.
All the time Mao Tse-tung laughing.
He takes heaps of money.
He laughs and he gives it to Krushchev.

Chairman Mao's belongings on the March:
"Two cotton and wool mixture blankets,
A sheet, two pants and jackets,
A sweater
A patched umbrella
An enamel mug for a rice bowl
A gray brief-case with nine pockets."

Like Han-shan standing there
    —a rubbing off some cliff
Hair sticking out smiling
    maybe rolling a homegrown
    Yenan cigarette
Took a crack at politics
The world is all one.
    —crawling out that hillside cave dirt house—

(whatever happened to Wong—
quit Chinese school, slugged his dad
left the laundry, went to sea
out the golden gate—did he make AB?—)

black eggshell-thin
pots of Lung-shan
maybe three thousand years B C

You have killed
I saw the Tibetans just down from the passes
Limping in high felt boots
Sweating in furs
Flatland heat.
      and from Almora gazing at Trisul
      the new maps from Peking
      call it all China
      clear down to here, & the Gangetic plain—

From the Hongkong N.T. on a pine rise
See the other side: stub fields.
Geese, ducks, and children
      far off cries.
Down the river, tiny men
Walk a plank—maybe loading
                little river boat.
Is that China
Flat, brown, and wide?

The ancestors
what did they leave us.
K'ung fu-tze, some buildings, remain.
  —tons of soil gone.

Mountains turn desert.
Stone croppt flood, strippt hills,
The useless wandering river mouths,
Salt swamps
Silt on the floor of the sea.

Wind-borne glacial flour—
Ice-age of Europe,
Dust storms from Ordos to Finland
The loess of Yenan.
  glaciers
     "shrink
  and vanish like summer clouds . . ."

CROSS THE SNOWY MOUNTAIN
WE SHALL SEE CHAIRMAN MAO!

The year the long march started I was four.
How long has this gone on.
Rivers to wade, mountains to cross—
Chas. Leong showed me how to hold my chopsticks
      like the brush—
Upstairs a chinese restaurant catty-corner
       from the police
Portland, oregon, nineteen fifty-one,
Yakima Indian horseman, hair black as crows.
   shovel shaped incisors,
    epicanthic fold.
Misty peaks and cliffs of the Columbia,
Old loggers vanish in the rocks.
They wouldn't tote me rice and soy-sauce
      cross the dam
"Snyder you gettin just like
  a damned Chinaman."

Gambling with the Wasco and the Wishram
By the river under Hee Hee Butte
& bought a hard round loaf of weird bread
From a bakery in a tent
In a camp of Tibetans
At Bodh-Gaya
Where Gautama used to stay.

On hearing Joan Baez singing "East Virginia"
    Those were the days.
    we strolled under blossoming cherries
    ten acres of orchard
    holding hands, kissing,
    in the evening talkt Lenin and Marx.
You had just started out for Beijing.

    I slippt my hand under her blouse
    and undid her brassiere.
    I passt my hand over her breasts
    her sweet breath, it was too warm for May.
    I thought how the whole world
    my love, could love like this;
    blossoms, the books, revolution
    more trees, strong girls, clear springs;
You took Beijing
Chairman Mao, you should quit smoking.
    Dont bother those philosophers
Build dams, plant trees,
    dont kill flies by hand.
Marx was another westerner.
    it's all in the head.
You dont need the bomb.
    stick to farming.
Write some poems. Swim the river.

those blue overalls are great.
Dont shoot me, let's go drinking.
      just
Wait.

Twelve Hours out of New York
after Twenty-five Days at Sea

The sun always setting behind us.
I did not mean to come this far.
  —baseball games on the radio
    commercials that turn your hair—
The last time I saild this coast
Was nineteen forty eight
Washing galley dishes
    reading Gide in French.
In the rucksack I've got three *nata*
Handaxes from central Japan;
The square blade found in China
    all the way back to Stone—
A novel by Kafu NAGAI
About geisha in nineteen-ten
With a long thing about gardens
And how they change through the year;
Azalea ought to be blooming
    in the yard in Kyoto now.
Now we are north of Cape Hatteras
Tomorrow docking at eight.
    mop the deck round the steering gear,
Pack your stuff and get paid.

19.IV.1964

19

Through the Smoke Hole

for Don Allen

I

There is another world above this one; or outside of this one; the
way to it is thru the smoke of this one, & the hole that smoke
goes through. The ladder is the way through the smoke hole;
the ladder holds up, some say, the world above; it might have
been a tree or pole; I think it is merely a way.

Fire is at the foot of the ladder. The fire is in the center. The
walls are round. There is also another world below or inside
this one. The way there is down thru smoke. It is not neces-
sary to think of a series.

Raven and Magpie do not need the ladder. They fly thru the
smoke holes shrieking and stealing. Coyote falls thru; we
recognize him only as a clumsy relative, a father in old clothes
we don't wish to see with our friends.

It is possible to cultivate the fields of our own world without
much thought for the others. When men emerge from below
we see them as the masked dancers of our magic dreams.
When men disappear down, we see them as plain men go-
ing somewhere else. When men disappear up we see them as
great heroes shining through the smoke. When men come
back from above they fall thru and tumble; we don't really
know them; Coyote, as mentioned before.

II

Out of the kiva come
masked dancers or

plain men.
    plain men go into the ground.

out there out side all the chores
    wood and water, dirt,
wind, the view across the flat,
here, in the round
                    no corners
head is full of magic figures—
woman your secrets aren't my secrets
what I cant say I wont
walk round
put my hand flat down.
you in the round too.
gourd vine blossom.
walls and houses drawn up
from the same soft soil.
thirty million years gone
        drifting sand.
    cool rooms pink stone
worn down fort floor, slat sighting
    heat shine on jumna river

dry wash, truck tracks in the riverbed
coild sand pinyon.

        seabottom
        riverbank
        sand dunes
the floor of a sea once again.

        human fertilizer
        underground water tunnels
        skinny dirt gods
        grandmother berries

out
through the smoke hole.
    (for childhood and youth *are* vanity)

a Permian reef of algae,

out through the smoke hole
swallowed sand
            salt mud
swum bodies,   flap
to the limestone blanket—

lizzard tongue,   lizzard tongue

    wha, wha, wha   flying
in and *out* thru the smoke hole

            plain men
    come out of the ground.

Song of the Taste

Eating the living germs of grasses
Eating the ova of large birds

    the fleshy sweetness packed
    around the sperm of swaying trees

The muscles of the flanks and thighs of
              soft-voiced cows
    the bounce in the lamb's leap
    the swish in the ox's tail

Eating roots grown swoll
         inside the soil

Drawing on life of living
    clustered points of light spun
         out of space
hidden in the grape.

Eating each other's seed
         eating
  ah, each other.

Kissing the lover in the mouth of bread:
        lip to lip.

Kyoto Born in Spring Song

Beautiful little children
     found in melons,
     in bamboo,
in a "strangely glowing warbler egg"
     a perfect baby girl—

baby, baby,
   tiny precious
      mice and worms:

  Great majesty of Dharma turning
  Great dance of Vajra power

lizard baby by the fern
centipede baby scrambling toward the wall
cat baby left to mew for milk alone
mouse baby too afraid to run

    O sing   born in spring
the weavers swallows babies in Nishijin
    nests below the eaves

    glinting mothers wings
    swoop to the sound of looms

    and three fat babies
  with three human mothers
every morning doing laundry
          "good
morning how's your baby?"
Tomoharu, Itsuko, and Kenji—

Mouse, begin again.

Bushmen are laughing
    at the coyote-tricking
        that made us think machines

    wild babies
in the ferns and plums and weeds.

Shark Meat

In the night fouled the nets—
Sonoyama's flying-fish fishing
Speared by the giant trident
        that hung in the net shed
            we never thought used

Cut up for meat on the beach.
At seven in the morning
Maeda's grandson
                the shy one
                —a slight harelip
Brought a crescent of pale red flesh
        two feet long, looped on his arm
Up the bamboo lanes to our place.

The island eats shark meat at noon.

Sweet miso sauce on a big boiled cube
        as I lift a flake

                to my lips

Miles of water, Black current,
Thousands of days
      re-crossing his own paths
      to tangle our net
            to be part of
            this loom.

The Bed in the Sky

Motorcycle strums   the empty streets
Heading home at one a.m.
    ice slicks shine in the moon
            I weave a safe path through

Naked shivering light flows down
Fills the basin over Kyoto
      and the plain
            a ghost glacier dream

From here a hundred miles are clear
the cemetery behind
      Namu   Amida   Butsu
            chiselled   ten thousand times

Tires crackle the mud-puddles
The northern hills gleam white
    I ought to stay outside   alone
            and watch the moon all night

But the bed is full and spread and dark
I hug you and sink in the warm

my stomach against your big belly

feels our baby turn

Revolution in the Revolution
in the Revolution

The country surrounds the city
The back country surrounds the country

"From the masses to the masses" the most
Revolutionary consciousness is to be found
Among the most ruthlessly exploited classes:
Animals, trees, water, air, grasses

We must pass through the stage of the
"Dictatorship of the Unconscious" before we can
Hope for the withering-away of the states
And finally arrive at true Communionism.

If the capitalists and imperialists
        are the exploiters, the masses are the workers.
                and the party
                is the communist.

If civilization
        is the exploiter, the masses is nature.
                and the party
                is the poets.

If the abstract rational intellect
        is the exploiter, the masses is the unconscious.
            and the party
            is the yogins.

& POWER
comes out of the seed-syllables of mantras.

In the Night, Friend

Peach blossom
Cling Peaches
Freestone peach.

The Third Engineer meets my wife in the pantry
says "Beards don't make money"
says "I've got two cars"

        (At thirty-five my father had a wife,
        two children, two acres, and two cows.
        he built a barn, fixed the house and added on,
        strung barbed-wire fence,
        planted fruit-trees, blasted stumps,
        they always had a car.
        they thought they were poor—   1935—)

—"the money culture run by Jews"
—"the Africans got all they know from us"

        Etchings of ruins,
        "Interno del Colosseo Scavato nel 1813"
        —Rossini—Roma—1820—
        hung in the passenger lounge.

Fruit tree fields.   orchards.   Santa Clara, San Jose.
      trailer parks in the lemon groves.
Seaman with a few extra bucks:
Talks of stocks, talks of taxes, buy up land.
      the whole state of California
      layed out like meat on a slab.
Growth and investment; development and returns.
—"I think them poets are all just charlatans."

says Dōgen, "every one of us
                    has a natural endowment
                    with provisions for the whole of his life."

Off the coast of Oregon
The radio is full of hate and anger.
"Teenagers! getting busted for shoplifting is no joke!"
      phoney friendly cop voice,
"The Ford Foundation is financing revolution—"
"Teach black people to have more self-respect
      and they'll blame the white people more—"

> General Alarm
> When Bell Rings
> Go to Your
> Station

After midnight, the "clean time of night"
Rise to see the Morning Star.
Planting the peach tree, mopping the floor.

> "we all
> worked hard to get ahead"
> peach orchard turned roots-up and brush-piled
> (the unspeakable U S government
> cut down the Navajo peach trees
> at Canyon de Chelly—)

On the face of the waters
A wind moves
Making waves

In the dark
Is a face

Of waters.

A wind moves
Like a word

waves

The face
Is a ground
Land
Looks round

SS Washington Bear
West Coast bound

Running Water Music II

Clear running stream
            clear running stream

Your water is light
            to my mouth
And a light to my dry body

            your flowing
Music,
            in my ears. free,

Flowing free!
With you
            in me.

from
Turtle Island (1974)

Control Burn

What the Indians
here
used to do, was,
to burn out the brush every year.
in the woods, up the gorges,
keeping the oak and the pine stands
tall and clear
with grasses
and kitkitdizze under them,
never enough fuel there
that a fire could crown.

Now, manzanita,
(a fine bush in its right)
crowds up under the new trees
mixed up with logging slash
and a fire can wipe out all.

Fire is an old story.
I would like,
with a sense of helpful order,
with respect for laws
of nature,
to help my land
with a burn. a hot clean
burn.
        (manzanita seeds will only open

after a fire passes over
or once passed through a bear)

And then
it would be more
like,
when it belonged to the Indians

Before.

Prayer for the Great Family

Gratitude to Mother Earth, sailing through night and day—
    and to her soil: rich, rare, and sweet
        in our minds so be it.

Gratitude to Plants, the sun-facing light-changing leaf
    and fine root-hairs; standing still through wind
    and rain; their dance is in the flowing spiral grain
        in our minds so be it.

Gratitude to Air, bearing the soaring Swift and the silent
    Owl at dawn. Breath of our song
    clear spirit breeze
        in our minds so be it.

Gratitude to Wild Beings, our brothers, teaching secrets,
    freedoms, and ways; who share with us their milk;
    self-complete, brave, and aware
        in our minds so be it.

Gratitude to Water: clouds, lakes, rivers, glaciers;
    holding or releasing; streaming through all
    our bodies salty seas
            in our minds so be it.

Gratitude to the Sun: blinding pulsing light through
    trunks of trees, through mists, warming caves where
    bears and snakes sleep—he who wakes us—
            in our minds so be it.

Gratitude to the Great Sky
    who holds billions of stars—and goes yet beyond that—
    beyond all powers, and thoughts
    and yet is within us—
    Grandfather Space.
    The Mind is his Wife.

            so be it.

                            after a Mohawk prayer

Facts

1. 92% of Japan's three million ton import of soybeans comes
from the U.S.

2. The U.S. has 6% of the world's population; consumes 1/3 the
energy annually consumed in the world.

3. The U.S. consumes 1/3 of the world's annual meat.

4. The top 1/5 of American population gets 45% of salary income, and owns about 77% of the total wealth. The top 1% owns 20 to 30% of personal wealth.

5. A modern nation needs 13 basic industrial raw materials. By AD 2000 the U.S. will be import-dependent on all but phosphorus.

6. General Motors is bigger than Holland.

7. Nuclear energy is mainly subsidized with fossil fuels and barely yields net energy.

8. The "Seven Sisters"—Exxon, Mobil, Texaco, Gulf, Standard of California, British Petroleum, Royal Dutch Shell.

9. "The reason solar energy has not and will not be a major contributor or substitute for fossil fuels is that it will not compete without energy subsidy from fossil fuel economy. The plants have already maximized the use of sunlight." —H. T. Odum

10. Our primary source of food is the sun.

The Uses of Light

It warms my bones
      say the stones

I take it into me and grow
Say the trees
Leaves above

Roots below

A vast vague white
Draws me out of the night
Says the moth in his flight—

Some things I smell
Some things I hear
And I see things move
Says the deer—

A high tower
on a wide plain.
If you climb up
One floor
You'll see a thousand miles more.

The Wild Mushroom

Well the sunset rays are shining
Me and Kai have got our tools
A basket and a trowel
And a book with all the rules

Don't ever eat Boletus
If the tube-mouths they are red
Stay away from the Amanitas

41

Or brother you are dead

Sometimes they're already rotten
Or the stalks are broken off
Where the deer have knocked them over
While turning up the duff

We set out in the forest
To seek the wild mushroom
In shapes diverse and colorful
Shining through the woodland gloom

If you look out under oak trees
Or around an old pine stump
You'll know a mushroom's coming
By the way the leaves are humped

They send out multiple fibers
Through the roots and sod
Some make you mighty sick they say
Or bring you close to God

So here's to the mushroom family
A far-flung friendly clan
For food, for fun, for poison
They are a help to man.

The Hudsonian Curlew

for Drum and Diana

The end of a desert track—turnaround—
    parked the truck and walked over dunes.
a cobbly point   hooks in the shallow bay;

      the Mandala of birds.

pelican, seagulls, and terns,
        one curlew
        far at the end—
they fly up as they see us
          and settle back down.
tern keep coming
        —skies of wide seas—
frigate birds keep swooping

pelicans sit nearest the foam;

tern bathing and fluttering
      in frothy wave-lapping
        between the round stones.

      we
gather driftwood for firewood
for camping
get four shells to serve up steamed snail

      in the top of the cardón cactus
      two vultures
      look, yawn, hunch, preen.
      out on the point   the seabirds

43

squabble and settle, meet and leave;
               speak.

two sides of a border.
the margins.   tidewater.   zones.
up in the void,   under the surface,
two worlds   touch
and greet

Three shotgun shots as it gets dark;
two birds.
       "how come three shots?"
       "one went down on the water
       and started to swim.
       I didn't want another thing like that duck."

the bill curved in, and the long neck limp—
a grandmother plumage of cinnamon and brown.
the beak not so long—bars on the head;
       by the eye.
       Hudsonian Curlew

           and those tern most likely
           "Royal Tern"
           with forked tail,
           that heavy orange bill.

The down
i pluck from the
neck of the curlew
eddies and whirls at my knees

in the twilight wind
from sea
kneeling in sand

warm in the hand.

"Do you want to do it right? I'll tell you."
he tells me.
at the edge of the water on the stones.
a transverse cut just below the sternum
the forefinger and middle finger
     forced in and up, following the
     curve of the rib cage.
then fingers arched, drawn slowly down and back,
forcing all the insides up and out,
toward the palm and heel of the hand.
firm organs, well-placed, hot.
save the liver;
finally scouring back, toward the vent, the last of the
     large intestine.

the insides string out, begin to wave, in the lapping
     waters of the bay.
the bird has no feathers, head, or feet;
     he is empty inside.
the rich body muscle that he moved by, the wing-beating
     muscle
anchored to the blade-like high breast bone,
is what you eat.

The black iron frying pan on the coals.
two birds singed in flame.
bacon, onion, and garlic
browning, then steaming with a lid
put the livers in,
half a bird apiece and bulghour
passed about the fire on metal plates.
dense firm flesh,
dark and rich,
          gathered news of skies and seas.

at dawn
looking out from the dunes
no birds at all but
three curlew

          ker-lew!

          ker-lew!

pacing   and glancing   around.

Baja: Bahía de Concepción, '69

Why Log Truck Drivers Rise
Earlier than Students of Zen

In the high seat, before-dawn dark,
Polished hubs gleam
And the shiny diesel stack

Warms and flutters
Up the Tyler Road grade
To the logging on Poorman creek.
Thirty miles of dust.

There is no other life.

Magpie's Song

Six A.M.,
Sat down on excavation gravel
by juniper and desert S.P. tracks
interstate 80 not far off
        between trucks
Coyotes—maybe three
            howling and yapping from a rise.

Magpie on a bough
Tipped his head and said,

> *"Here in the mind, brother*
> *Turquoise blue.*
> *I wouldn't fool you.*
> *Smell the breeze*
> *It came through all the trees*
> *No need to fear*
> *What's ahead*
> *Snow up on the hills west*
> *Will be there every year*
> *be at rest.*

A feather on the ground—
The wind sound—

Here in the Mind, Brother,
Turquoise Blue"

Dusty Braces

O you ancestors
lumber schooners
       big moustache
long-handled underwear
sticks out under the cuffs

tan stripes on each shoulder,
dusty braces—
    nine bows
    nine bows
you bastards
my fathers
and grandfathers, stiff-necked
punchers, miners, dirt farmers, railroad-men

killed off the cougar and grizzly

nine bows. You itch
in my boots too,

—your sea roving
tree hearted son.

For the Children

The rising hills, the slopes,
of statistics
lie before us.
the steep climb
of everything, going up,
up, as we all
go down.

In the next century
or the one beyond that,
they say,
are valleys, pastures,
we can meet there in peace
if we make it.

To climb these coming crests
one word to you, to
you and your children:

stay together
learn the flowers
go light

As for Poets

As for poets
The Earth Poets
Who write small poems,
Need help from no man.

The Air Poets
Play out the swiftest gales
And sometimes loll in the eddies.
Poem after poem,
Curling back on the same thrust.

At fifty below
Fuel oil won't flow
And propane stays in the tank.
Fire Poets
Burn at absolute zero
Fossil love pumped back up.

The first
Water Poet
Stayed down six years.
He was covered with seaweed.
The life in his poem
Left millions of tiny

Different tracks
Criss-crossing through the mud.

With the Sun and Moon
In his belly,
The Space Poet
Sleeps.
No end to the sky—
But his poems,
Like wild geese,
Fly off the edge.

A Mind Poet
Stays in the house.
The house is empty
And it has no walls.
The poem
Is seen from all sides,
Everywhere,
At once.

from
Myths & Texts (1978)

Logging

8

Each dawn is clear
Cold air bites the throat.
Thick frost on the pine bough
Leaps from the tree
    snapped by the diesel

Drifts and glitters in the
      horizontal sun.
In the frozen grass
       smoking boulders
       ground by steel tracks.
In the frozen grass
      wild horses stand
      beyond a row of pines.
The D8 tears through piss-fir,
Scrapes the seed-pine
           chipmunks flee,
A black ant carries an egg
Aimlessly from the battered ground.
Yellowjackets swarm and circle
Above the crushed dead log, their home.
Pitch oozes from barked
      trees still standing,
Mashed bushes make strange smells.
Lodgepole pines are brittle.
Camprobbers flutter to watch.

A few stumps, drying piles of brush;
Under the thin duff, a toe-scrape down
Black lava of a late flow.
Leaves stripped from thornapple
Taurus by nightfall.

10

A ghost logger wanders a shadow
In the early evening, boots squeak
With the cicada, the fleas
Nest warm in his blanket-roll
Berrybrambles catch at the stagged pants
He stumbles up the rotted puncheon road
There is a logging camp
Somewhere in there among the alders
Berries and high rotting stumps
Bindlestiff with a wooden bowl
(The poor bastards at Nemi in the same boat)
What old Seattle skidroad did he walk from
Fifty years too late, and all his
                              money spent?

Dogfish and Shark oil
Greasing the skids.
"Man is the heart of the universe
the upshot of the five elements,
born to enjoy food and color and noise ..."
Get off my back Confucius
There's enough noise now.
What bothers me is all those stumps:
What did they do with the wood?
Them Xtians out to save souls and grab land
"They'd steal Christ off the cross

                    if he wasn't nailed on"
The last decent carpentry
Ever done by Jews.

15

Lodgepole
            cone/seed waits for fire
And then thin forests of silver-gray.
            in the void
            a pine cone falls
Pursued by squirrels
What mad pursuit! What struggle to escape!

Her body a seedpod
Open to the wind
"A seed pod void of seed
We had no meeting together"
            so you and I must wait
Until the next blaze
Of the world, the universe,
Millions of worlds, burning
            —oh let it lie.

Shiva at the end of the kalpa:
Rock-fat, hill-flesh, gone in a whiff.
Men who hire men to cut groves
Kill snakes, build cities, pave fields,
Believe in god, but can't
Believe their own senses
Let alone Gautama. Let them lie.

Pine sleeps, cedar splits straight
Flowers crack the pavement.

Pa-ta Shan-jen
(A painter who watched Ming fall)
            lived in a tree:
"The brush
May paint the mountains and streams
Though the territory is lost."

Hunting

11

songs for a four-crowned dancing hat

O Prajapati
              You who floated on the sea
              Hatched to godhead in the slime
Heated red and beaten for a bronze ritual bowl
The Boar!
              Dripping boar emerged
              On his tusk his treasure
Prajapati from the sea-depths:
Skewered body of the earth
Each time I carry you this way.

The year I wore my Raven skin
   Dogfish ran. Too many berries on the hill
Grizzly fat and happy in the sun—
   The little women, the fern women,
They have stopped crying now.
   "What will you do with human beings?
Are you going to save the human beings?"
   That was Southeast, they say.

12

Out the Greywolf valley
in late afternoon
after eight days in the high meadows
hungry, and out of food,
the trail broke into a choked
clearing, apples grew gone wild
hung on one low bough by a hornet's nest.
caught the drone in tall clover
lowland smell in the shadows
then picked a hard green one:
watched them swarm.
smell of the mountains still on me.
none stung.

15

First day of the world.
White rock ridges
                          new born
Jay chatters   the first time
Rolling a smoke by the campfire
New! never before.
                          bitter coffee, cold
Dawn wind, sun on the cliffs,
You'll find it in *Many old shoes*
High!   high on poetry & mountains.

That silly ascetic Gautama
           thought he knew something;
Maudgalyâyana   knew hell
Knew every hell, from the
Cambrian to the Jurassic
He suffered in them all.

16

How rare to be born a human being!
Wash him off with cedar-bark and milkweed
            send the damned doctors home.
Baby, baby, noble baby
Noble-hearted baby

One hand up, one hand down
"I alone am the honored one"
Birth of the Buddha.
And the whole world-system trembled.
"If that baby really said that,
I'd cut him up and throw him to the dogs!"
said Chao-chou the Zen Master. But
Chipmunks, gray squirrels, and
Golden-mantled ground squirrels
            brought him each a nut.
Truth being the sweetest of flavors.

Girls would have in their arms
A wild gazelle or wild wolf-cubs
And give them their white milk,
            those who had new-born infants home
Breasts still full.
Wearing a spotted fawnskin
            sleeping under trees
            bacchantes, drunk
On wine or truth, what you will,
Meaning: compassion.
Agents: man and beast, beasts
Got the buddha-nature
All but
Coyote.

Burning

9

Night here,   a covert
All spun, webs in one
        how without grabbing hold it?
—Get into the bird-cage
        without starting them singing.

"Forming the New Society
        Within the shell of the Old"
The motto in the Wobbly Hall
Some old Finns and Swedes playing cards
Fourth and Yesler in Seattle.
O you modest, retiring, virtuous young ladies
        pick the watercress, pluck the yarrow
"Kwan kwan" goes the crane in the field,
        I'll meet you tomorrow;
A million workers dressed in black and buried,
We make love in leafy shade.

Bodhidharma sailing the Yangtze on a reed
Lenin in a sealed train through Germany
Hsüan Tsang, crossing the Pamirs
Joseph, Crazy Horse, living the last free
        starving high-country winter of their tribes.
Surrender into freedom, revolt into slavery—
Confucius no better—

         (with Lao-tzu to keep him in check)
"Walking about the countryside
                all one fall
To a heart's content beating on stumps."

15

Stone-flake and salmon.
The pure, sweet, straight-splitting
                        with a ping
Red cedar of the thick coast valleys
Shake-blanks on the mashed ferns
                        the charred logs
Fireweed and bees
An old burn, by new alder
Creek on smooth stones,
Back there a Tarheel logger farm.
(High country fir still hunched in snow)

From Siwash strawberry-pickers in the Skagit
Down to the boys at Sac,
Living by the river
                riding flatcars to Fresno,
Across the whole country
Steep towns, flat towns, even New York,
And oceans and Europe & libraries & galleries
And the factories they make rubbers in
This whole spinning show
                (among others)
Watched by the Mt. Sumeru L. O.

From the middle of the universe
& them with no radio.
"What is imperfect is best"

　　　　　silver scum on the trout's belly
　　　　　rubs off on your hand.
It's all falling or burning—
　　　　　rattle of boulders
　　　　　steady dribbling of rocks down cliffs
　　　　　bark chips in creeks
Porcupine chawed here—
　　　　　　　　Smoke
From Tillamook a thousand miles
Soot and hot ashes. Forest fires.
Upper Skagit burned I think 1919
Smoke covered all northern Washington.
　　　　　lightning strikes, flares,
Blossoms a fire on the hill.
Smoke like clouds. Blotting the sun
Stinging the eyes.
The hot seeds steam underground
　　　　　still alive

16

"Wash me on home, mama"
　　　　　　—song of the Kelp.
A chief's wife
Sat with her back to the sun
On the sandy beach, shredding cedar-bark.
Her fingers were slender
She didn't eat much.

"Get foggy
We're going out to dig
Buttercup roots"

Dream, Dream,

Earth! those beings living on your surface
none of them disappearing, will all be transformed.
When I have spoken to them
when they have spoken to me, from that moment on,
their words and their bodies which they
usually use to move about with, will all change.
I will not have heard them. Signed,

(   )

Coyote

17

the text
Sourdough mountain called a fire in:
Up Thunder Creek, high on a ridge.
Hiked eighteen hours, finally found
A snag and a hundred feet around on fire:
All afternoon and into night
Digging the fire line
Falling the burning snag
It fanned sparks down like shooting stars
Over the dry woods, starting spot-fires
Flaring in wind up Skagit valley
From the Sound.
Toward morning it rained.
We slept in mud and ashes,
Woke at dawn, the fire was out,
The sky was clear, we saw
The last glimmer of the morning star.

the myth
Fire up Thunder Creek and the mountain—
troy's burning!
The cloud mutters
The mountains are your mind.
The woods bristle there,

Dogs barking and children shrieking
Rise from below.

Rain falls for centuries
Soaking the loose rocks in space
Sweet rain, the fire's out
The black snag glistens in the rain
& the last wisp of smoke floats up
Into the absolute cold
Into the spiral whorls of fire
The storms of the Milky Way
"Buddha incense in an empty world"
Black pit cold and light-year
Flame tongue of the dragon
Licks the sun

The sun is but a morning star

Crater Mt. L.O. 1952-Marin-an 1956

end of myths & texts

Lookout's Journal

A. Crater Mountain

22 June 52   Marblemount Ranger Station
            Skagit District, Mt. Baker National Forest

Hitchhiked here, long valley of the Skagit. Old cars parked in the weeds, little houses in fields of bracken. A few cows, in stumpland.

Ate at the "parkway café" real lemon in the pie
       "—why don't you get a jukebox in here"
       "—the man said we weren't important enough"

— — — —

28 June

                    Blackie Burns:
"28 years ago you could find a good place to fish.
GREEDY & SELFISH   NO RESPECT FOR THE
   LAND
       tin cans, beer bottles, dirty dishes
       a shit within a foot of the bed
one sonuvabitch out of fifty

fishguts in the creek
the door left open for the bear.

If you're takin forestry fellas keep away
from the recreation side of it:
first couple months you see the women you say
       'there's a cute little number'
the next three months it's only another woman
after that you see one coming out of the can
       & wonder if she's just shit on the floor

ought to use pit toilets"

— — — —

Granite creek Guard station   9 July

  the boulder in the creek never moves
      the water is always falling
    together!

A ramshackle little cabin built by Frank Beebe the miner.
Two days walk to here from roadhead.
        arts of the Japanese: moon-watching
                  insect-hearing
Reading the sutra of Hui Nêng.

  one does not need universities and libraries
  one need be alive to what is about

saying "I don't care"

— — — —

11 July

cut fresh rhubarb by the bank
the creek is going down

last night caught a trout
today climbed to the summit of Crater Mountain and back
high and barren: flowers I don't recognize
ptarmigan and chicks, feigning the broken wing.

    Baxter: "Men are funny, once I loved a girl
    so bad it hurt, but I drove her away. She was
    throwing herself at me—and four months later she
    married another fellow."

A doe in the trail, unafraid.
A strange man walking south
A boy from Marblemount with buckteeth, learning machine shop.

— — — —

Crater Mountain   Elevation: 8049 feet   23 July

Really wretched weather for three days now—wind, hail, sleet,
snow; the FM transmitter is broken / rather the receiver is /
what can be done?

    Even here, cold foggy rocky place, there's life—4 ptarmigan
by the A-frame, cony by the trail to the snowbank.

    hit my head on the lamp,
    the shutters fall, the radio quits,
    the kerosene stove won't stop, the wood stove
    won't start, my fingers are too numb to write.

& this is mid-July. At least I have energy enough to read science-fiction. One has to go to bed fully clothed.

— — — —

The stove burning wet wood—windows misted over giving the blank white light of shoji. Outside wind blows, no visibility. I'm filthy with no prospect of cleaning up. (Must learn yoga-system of Patanjali—)

— — — —

Crater Shan   28 July

    Down for a new radio, to Ross Lake, and back up. Three days walking. Strange how unmoved this place leaves one; neither articulate or worshipful; rather the pressing need to look within and adjust the mechanism of perception.

A dead sharp-shinned hawk, blown by the wind against the lookout. Fierce compact little bird with a square head.

—If one wished to write poetry of nature, where an audience? Must come from the very conflict of an attempt to articulate the vision   poetry & nature in our time.

> (reject the human; but the tension of
> human events, brutal and tragic, against
> a non-human background? like Jeffers?)

— — — —

Pair of eagles soaring over Devil's Creek canyon

– – – –

31 July

This morning:
>   floating face down in the water bucket
>   a drowned mouse.

"Were it not for Kuan Chung, we should be wearing our hair
unbound and our clothes buttoning on the left side"

>   A man should stir himself with poetry
>   Stand firm in ritual
>   Complete himself in music
>   lun yü

– – – –

Comparing the panoramic Lookout View photo dated 8 August
1935: with the present view. Same snowpatches; same shapes.
Year after year; snow piling up and melting.

>   "By God" quod he, "for pleynly, at a word
>   Thy drasty ryming is not worth a tord."

– – – –

Crater Shan   3 August

How pleasant to squat in the sun
Jockstrap & zoris

73

form—leaving things out at the right spot
ellipse, is emptiness

                              these ice-scoured valleys
                            swarming with plants
   "I am the Queen Bee!
                       Follow Me"

                 – – – –

Or having a wife and baby,
   living close to the ocean, with skills for
   gathering food.

QUEBEC DELTA 04 BLACK

Higgins to Pugh (over)
   "the wind comes out of the east
     or northeast,
     the chimney smokes all over the room.
     the wind comes out of the west;
     the fire burns clean."

Higgins L.O. reads the news:
   "flying saucer with a revolving black band
     drouth in the south.
Are other worlds watching us?"
The rock alive,   not barren.
     flowers   lichen   pinus albicaulis   chipmunks
mice   even grass.

—first I turn on the radio
—then make tea & eat breakfast
—study Chinese until eleven

—make lunch, go chop snow to melt for water,
read Chaucer in the early afternoon.

> "Is this real
>   Is this real
>   This life I am living?"
> > —Tlingit or Haida song

— — — —

"Hidden Lake to Sourdough"
—"This is Sourdough"
—"Whatcha doing over there?"
—"Readin some old magazines
            they had over here."

— — — —

6 August

Clouds above and below, but I can see Kulshan, Mt. Terror,
Shuksan; they blow over the ridge between here and
Three-fingered Jack, fill up the valleys. The Buckner Boston
Peak ridge is clear.

What happens all winter; the wind driving snow; clouds—
wind, and mountains—repeating

        this is what always happens here,

and the photograph of a young female torso hung in the lookout
window, in the foreground. Natural against natural, beauty.

                two butterflies

                    a chilly clump of mountain
                              flowers

zazen   non-life.   An art: mountain-watching.

        leaning in the doorway whistling
            a chipmunk popped out
                  listening

                    — — — —

9 August

Sourdough: Jack, do you know if a fly is an electrical
    conductor? (over)
Desolation: A fly? Are you still trying to electrocute flies? (over)
Sourdough: Yeah   I can make em twitch a little. I got five
    number six batteries on it (over)
Desolation: I don't know, Shubert, keep trying. Desolation
    clear.

                    — — — —

10 August

    First wrote a haiku and painted a haiga for it; then repaired
the Om Mani Padme Hum prayer flag, then constructed a stone
platform, then shaved down a shake and painted a zenga on it,
then studied the lesson.

            a butterfly
                scared up from its flower
        caught by the wind and swept over the cliffs
                              SCREE

                              76

Vaux Swifts: in great numbers, flying before the storm,
arcing so close that the sharp wing-whistle is heard.

                    "The śrāvaka
disciplined in Tao, enlightened, but on the wrong path."
summer,
            on the west slopes creek beds are brushy
            north-faces of ridges, steep and
                    covered late with snow

            slides and old burns on dry hills.

(In San Francisco: I live on the Montgomery Street drainage
—at the top of a long scree slope just below a cliff.)

                    — — — —

sitting in the sun in the doorway
picking my teeth with a broomstraw
listenin to the buzz of the flies.

                    — — — —

12 August

            A visit all day, to the sheep camp, across the
glacier and into Devil's park. A tent under a clump of Alpine
fir; horses, sheep in the meadow.

                    take up solitary occupations.

Horses stand patiently, rump to the wind.
                    —gave me one of his last two cigars.

Designs, under the shut lids, glowing in sun

        (experience!   that drug.)
Then the poor lonely lookouts, radioing forth and back.

After a long day's travel, reached the ridge,
followed a deer trail down
                to five small lakes.
in this yuga, the moral imperative is to COMMUNICATE.
Making tea.

fewer the artifacts, less the words,
             slowly the life of it
a knack for non-attachment.

Sourdough radioing to the smoke-chaser crew

"you're practically there
you gotta go up the cliff
you gotta cross the rock slide
look for a big blaze on a big tree
        [two climbers killed by lightning
         on Mt. Stuart]
"are you on the timber stand
or are you on the side of the cliff?
Say, Bluebell, where are you?
A patch of salmonberry and tag-alder to the right"
        —must take a look.

        — — — —

Cratershan 15 August

   When the mind is exhausted of images, it invents its own.

orange juice is what she asked for
    bright chrome restaurant, 2 a.m.
the rest of us drinking coffee
but the man brought orange pop.   haw!

late at night, the eyes tired, the teapot empty, the tobacco damp.

Almost had it last night: *no identity*. One thinks, "I emerged
from some general, non-differentiated thing, I return to it." One
has in reality never left it; there is no return.

                    my language fades.   Images of erosion.

"That which includes all change never changes; without change
time is meaningless; without time, space is destroyed. Thus we
arrive at the void."

                    — — — —

"If a Bodhisattva retains the thought of an ego, a person, a
being, or a soul, he is no more a Bodhisattva."

        You be Bosatsu,
        I'll be the taxi-driver
        Driving you home

The curious multi-stratified metamorphic rock. Blue and
white, clouds reaching out. To survive a winter here learn to
browse and live in holes in the rocks under snow.
Sabi: One does not have a great deal to give. That which one
does give has been polished and perfected into a spontaneous
emptiness; sterility made creative, it has no pretensions, and
encompasses everything.

                    Zen view, o.k.?

                    — — — —

79

21 August

Oiling and stowing the tools.   (artifact / tools: now there's
a topic.)
When a storm blows in, covering the south wall with rain and
blotting out the mountains. Ridges look new in every light. Still
discovering new conformations—every cony has an ancestry
but the rocks were just here.
Structure in the lithosphere / cycles of change in rock / only
the smallest percentage sanded and powdered and mixed with
life-derived elements.
Is chemical reaction a type of perception??—Running through
all things   motion and reacting, object against object / there is
more than enough time for all things to happen: swallowing
its own tail.

– – – –

Diablo Dam   24 August

Back down off Crater in a snowstorm, after closing up the
lookout. With Baxter from Granite Creek all the way to the
dam for more supplies. Clouds on the rocks, rain falls and
falls. Tomorrow we shall fill packs with food and return to
Granite Creek.

– – – –

In San Francisco: September 13.

Boys on bicycles in the asphalt playground wheeling and circling
aimlessly like playful gulls or swallows. Smell of a fresh-parked
car.

– – – –

B. Sourdough

Marblemount Ranger Station   27 June 53

The antique car managed it to Marblemount last week, and then
to Koma Kulshan for a week of gnats, rain, & noise.

The Philosophy of the Forest Service: Optimistic view of
nature—democratic, utilitarian "Nature is rational," Equals,
treat it right and it will make a billion board feet a year. Paradox
suppressed. What wd an Aristocratic F.S. be like? Man traps?

Forest equals crop / Scenery equals recreation / Public equals
money.   : : The shopkeeper's view of nature.

> Hail Mr. Pulaski, after whom the Pulaski
> Tool is named.

—the iron stove, the windows, and the trees. "It is, and is not, I
am sane enough." Get so you don't have to think about what
you're doing because you *know* what you're doing.

J. Francis: "Should I marry? It would mean a house; and the
next thirty years teaching school."   LOOKOUT!

Old McGuire and the fire of 1926:   40,000 acres on the
upper Skagit, a three-mile swathe. Going to scrub my clothes &
go down to Sedro-Woolley now with Jack.

– – – –

28 June

A day off—went to Bellingham and out to Gooseberry Bay, the
Lummi reservation. Past a shed with three long cedar canoes in

it. Finally to where the Lummi Island ferry stops, and this was about the end of the road, but we could drive a little farther on, and it was there we went through the Kitchen Midden. Through it, because the road cut right through shells and oysters and all. While looking at this a lady in a house shouted out to us; then came closer, & said if you're interested in the kitchen midden "as such" come out in back and "look where we had it bulldozed." And I said how do you like living on somebody's old kitchen heap, and she said it made her feel kind of funny sometimes. Then I said, well it's got about 3000 years in it vertical, but that might be dead wrong. It was 10 feet high, 45 feet wide, and 325 feet long, with one cedar stump on it about 110 years old, to show when (at least) it was finished with. Full of oyster, butter clam, cockle, mussel, snail and assorted shells.

We went back by the same road and at the outskirts of Bellingham Jack pointed out a ratty looking place called Coconut Grove where he said he had spent time drinking with a "rough crowd." They drank beer out of steins and called the place the Cat's Eye instead.

Outskirts of Bellingham, something of clear sky to the west over the waters of Puget Sound, the San Juan islands; and very black clouds up the Skagit, toward the vast mountain wilderness of the North Cascades. We turned off 99 to go into that black, wet hole, and it did start raining pretty quick after we went up that road. Coffee in Sedro-Woolley, a sign "No Drinks Served to Indians" and there are many Indians, being strawberry picking season, and Loggerodeo is next week. Marblemount Ranger Station about 8.30 & in the bunkhouse found a magazine with an article about an eighteen-year-old girl who could dance and paint and compose and sew and was good looking, too, with lots of pictures.

– – – –

Story: a Tarheel at Darrington had this nice dog. One day he
was out dynamiting fish—threw a stick of powder into the water,
all lit and ready to go. The dog jumped in, retrieved it, and ran
back with it in his mouth. The logger took off up a tree shouting
—Git back, Dog! Then it blasted. Tarheel still limps.
—Blackie.

—And then there was this young married couple, who stay
locked in their room four weeks—when friends finally break in
all they find is two assholes, jumping back and forth through
each other. " " "

– – – –

Ruby Creek Guard Station   30 June

The foamy wake behind the boat *does* look like the water of
Hokusai. Water in motion is precise and sharp, clearly formed,
holding specific postures for infinitely small frozen moments.
    Four mules: Tex, Barney Oldfield, Myrtle, Bluejay.
Four horses: Willy, Skeezix, Blaze, Mabel.

– – – –

Sourdough Mountain Lookout   Elevation: 5977 feet
17 July 53

"GREENEST Goddam kid I EVER saw. Told him he couldn't
boil beans at that altitude, he'd have to fry them. When I left
I said, now, be careful, this is something you gotta watch out
about, don't flog your dummy too much! And he says real
serious, Oh no, I won't. Hawww—"

"And then he was trying to fry an egg and he missed the pan and he missed the stove and landed the egg on both feet, he didn't know whether to run, shit, or go blind!"

Just managed to get through to Phil Whalen, on the radio, him up on Sauk Lookout now.

Rode up here on Willy the Paint, a pleasant white-eyed little horse that took great caution on rock and snow. Had to lead him across the whitewater at Sourdough Creek. Horses look noble from the side, but they sure are silly creatures when seen from the front. Mules just naturally silly—Whenever we stopped, Myrtle would commence kicking Bluejay & Bluejay would kick Barney, all with great WHACKS on the forkies, but Tex behaved, being neither kicked nor kicking. Shoeing Willy required the twitch, anvil, nails, three of us, and great sweating groaning and swearing. Blackie whacks him with a hammer while Roy twists his nose to make him be good.

This is the place to observe clouds and the gradual dissolution of snow. Chipmunk got himself locked in here and when I tried to shoo him out he'd just duck in a corner. Finally when I was sorting screws he came out and climbed up on the waterbucket looking I guess for a drink—hung on, face down, with his hind legs only to the edge of the pail, inside, for a long time, and finally fell in. Helped him out, splashing about—nobody been there he'd have drunned.

Keep looking across to Crater Mountain and get the funny feeling I am up there looking out, right now, "because there are no calendars in the mountains" —shifting of light & cloud, perfection of chaos, magnificent *jiji mu-ge* / interlacing interaction.

— — — —

Up at a quarter to six, wind still blowing the mist through the trees and over the snow. Rins'd my face in the waterhole at the edge of the snowfield—ringed with white rock and around that, heather. Put up the SX aerial on a long pole made by some lookout of years past, sticks & limbs & trunks all wired and tied together. Made a shelf for papers out of half an old orange crate, and turned the radio receiver off. Walked down the ridge, over the snow that follows so evenly the very crest—snow on the north slope, meadows and trees on the south. Small ponds, lying in meadows just off the big snowfields, snags, clumps of mountain hemlock, Alpine fir, a small amount of Alaska cedar.

Got back, built a fire and took the weather. About six, two bucks came, one three-point, one four-point, very warily, to nibble at huckleberries and oats and to eat the scraps of mouldy bacon I threw out. Shaggy and slender, right in the stiff wind blowing mist over the edge of the ridge, or out onto the snowfield, standing out clear and dark against the white. Clouds keep shifting—totally closed in; a moment later across to Pyramid Peak or up Thunder Creek it's clear. But the wind stays.

Now I've eaten dinner and stuffed the stove with twisted pitchy Alpine fir limbs. Clumps of trees fading into a darker and darker gray. White quartz veins on the rocks out the south window look like a sprinkling of snow. Cones on the top boughs of the Alpine fir at the foot of the rocks a DARK PURPLE, stand perfectly erect, aromatic clusters of LINGAMS fleshy and hard.

Lookout free talk time on the radio band: Saul called Koma Kulshan, Church called Sauk, Higgins is talking to Miner's Ridge. Time to light the lamp.

– – – –

23 July

Days mostly cloudy—clouds breaking up to let peaks through
once in a while. Logan, Buckner, Boston, Sahale, Snowpeak,
Pyramid, Névé, Despair, Terror, Fury, Challenger. And the
more distant Redoubt and Glacier Peak. As well as Hozomeen
and Three Fingered Jack. Right now looking down on the
Skagit—pink clouds—pale rose-water pink, with soft shadings of
gray and lavender, other combinations of pastel reds and
blues, hanging over Pyramid Peak.

Fretting with the Huang Po doctrine of Universal Mind. What
a thorny one.

– – – –

25 July

Last night: thunderstorm. A soft piling of cumulus over
the Little Beaver in late afternoon—a gradual thickening and
darkening. A brief shower of hail that passed over & went
up Thunder Creek valley: long gray shreds of it slowly falling
and bent in the wind—while directly above Ruby Creek
sunlight is streaming through. Velvety navy blue over Hozomeen,
with the sun going down behind Mt. Terror and brilliant
reds and pinks on the under-clouds, another red streak behind
black Hozomeen framed in dark clouds. Lightning moving
from Hozomeen slowly west into red clouds turning gray, then
black; rising wind. Sheet lightning pacing over Little Beaver,
fork lightning striking Beaver Pass.
    This morning a sudden heavy shower of rain and a thick
fog. A buck scared: ran off with stiff springy jumps down
the snowfield. Throwing sprays of snow with every leap:
head held stiffly high.

– – – –

9 August

Sourdough radio relay to Burns:

to: Ray Patterson, District Assistant, Early Winters
      Ranger Station.
from: Jud Longmoor.
  "Kit, Ted and Lucky went out over Deception Pass
  probably headed for airport. Belled but not
  hobbled. Horse took out in night, August 3, above
  Fish Camp. The Shull Creek trail is not passable now.
  Mt. Baker string will pack us to Skypilot Pass
  Thursday August 5. Have Ken Thompson meet us there
  with pack string and saddle horse for Loring. We
  will have pack gear and riding saddle."

Lightning Storm again: first in twilight the long jagged ones
back of Terror & Fury, later moving down Thunder Creek,
and then two fires: right after the strikes, red blooms in the
night. Clouds drifting in & obscuring them.

— — — —

   Discipline of self-restraint is an easy one; being clear-cut,
negative, and usually based on some accepted cultural values.
Discipline of following desires, *always* doing what you want to
do, is hardest. It presupposes self-knowledge of motives,
a careful balance of free action and sense of where the cultural
taboos lay—knowing whether a particular "desire" is instinctive,
cultural, personal, a product of thought, contemplation,
or the unconscious. Blake: if the doors of perception were
cleansed, everything would appear to man as it is, infinite. For
man has closed himself up, 'til all he sees is through narrow
chinks of his caverns. Ah.

the frustrate bumblebee turns over
clambers the flower's center upside down
furious hidden buzzing
near the cold sweet stem.

In a culture where the aesthetic experience is denied
and atrophied, genuine religious ecstasy rare, intellectual
pleasure scorned—it is only natural that sex should become
the only personal epiphany of most people & culture's
interest in romantic love take on staggering size.

The usefulness of hair on the legs: mosquitoes and
deerflies have to agitate it in drawing nigh the
skin—by that time warned—Death to Bugs.

(an empty water glass is no less empty than a universe
full of nothing)—the desk is under the pencil.

Sourdough Mountain Lookout   12 August

3:55 p.m.	Desolation calls in his weather.
4:00	Sourdough starts calling Marblemount.
4:00	Sam Barker asks for the air: "Dolly, call the doctor at Concrete and have him go up to Rockport. There's a man got hurt up here."
4:01	Marblemount: "Up where?"
4:01	Barker: "Up here on Sky Creek. A fellow from Stoddard's logging outfit."
4:01	Marblemount: "Okay Sam. Marblemount clear."
4:10	Sourdough calls his weather in to Marblemount.
4:11	Barker: "Dolly, did you make that call through?"

4:11	Marblemount "You mean for the doctor?"
4:12	Barker: "Yeah. Well the man's dead."
4:12	Marblemount: "Who was he?"
4:12	Barker: "I don't know, the one they call the Preacher."
4:13	Somebody I couldn't hear, calling Marblemount.
4:13	Marblemount: "The Sky Creek trail. I don't know. Somebody they call the Preacher." Marblemount clear.

— — — —

14 August

11:30 Hidden Lake spots a smoke; he hardly gets an azimuth
in to Marblemount but I've got it too & send my reading in.
Then all the other Lookouts in the North Cascades catch it—
a big column in the Baker River District, between Noisy
and Hidden Creeks.
So Phil on Sauk Mountain is busy calling Darrington and
Marblemount for the suppression crews, and then the patrol plane
comes to look at it and says it's about six acres of alpine
timber. & the trucks are off, and Willey the cook has to go too,
and the plane flies over to drop supplies at a fire-fighter's camp.

— — — —

Don't be a mountaineer, be a mountain.
        And shrug off a few with avalanches.

Sourdough Mountain at the hub of six valleys: Skagit,
Thunder, Ruby, Upper Skagit, Pierce Creek, Stetattle creek.

— — — —

20 August

Skirt blown against her hips, thighs, knees
        hair over her ears
    climbing the steep hill in high-heeled shoes

(the Deer come for salt, not affection)

—Government Confucianism, as in the *Hsiao-ching* / Filial
Piety—a devilish sort of liberalism. Allowing you should
give enough justice and food to prevent a revolution, yet surely
keeping the people under the thumb. "If you keep the taxes
just low enough, the people will not revolt, and you'll get rich."
Movements against this psychology—the Legalistic rule of
Ch'in; Wang An-shih perhaps?
        This is Chinese; plus Blake's collected,
Walden and sumi painting, pass the time.

— — — —

Nature a vast set of conventions, totally arbitrary, patterns
and stresses that come into being each instant; could disappear
totally anytime; and continues only as a form of play: the
cosmic / comic   delight.
        "For in this period the Poet's work is done
and all the great events of time start forth and are conceived in
such a period, within a moment, a Pulsation of the artery."
        —True insight a love-making hovering
between the void & the immense worlds of creation. To
symbolically represent Prajña as female is right. The
Prajña girl statue from Java.

— — — —

Old Roy Raymond hike up and see me. About noon I'm
chopping wood. We spend the afternoon playing horseshoes with
mule-shoes; this morning playing poker."
    "My Missus died a few years ago so I sold the house
    and the furniture 'til I got it down now to where I can get
    everything into a footlocker. My friends'd ask me
    What you sell that for, & hell, what use did I have for it?
    I'll never marry again."
So he spends his time in the mountains—construction
jobs, forestry, mining. Winters in Aberdeen.
    Kim on Desolation radios over (evenings) to read bits of
picturesque speech and patter from antique *Reader's Digests* he's
found chez Lookout.

– – – –

Ross Lake Guard Station   31 August

Friday morning with snow coming in and storms all
across the North Cascades, straight down from Canada,
Blackie radios to come down. Work all morning with
inventory; put the shutters down & had to pack an enormous
load of crap off the mountain. About 85 pounds.
    Forest Service float on Ross Lake: all on a big raft;
corrugated walls and roofing. Porch with woodpile. A floating
dock with crosscuts, falling saws, spikes, wood, in't. At one end
the green landing barge moored alongside. The main raft, with
a boat-size wood door; inside a tangle of tools, beds, groceries.
A vast Diesel marine engine-block in the middle of the deck with
a chainsaw beside it. Kim on a cot next to that. Shelves on the
unpainted wall with rice, coffee, pancake syrup. Cords, vices,
wires on the workbench. A screen cooler full of bacon and ham.

And this enters, under the same roof, into another dock-room in
which the patrol boat floats, full of green light from the water.
Around the edge bales of hay and drums of Diesel. Moored
alongside outside, the horse raft. Covered with straw and
manure. A sunny windy day, lapping the logs.

— — — —

Trail crew work up Big Beaver Creek   4 September

   Crosscutting a very large down cedar across the trail and
then wedging, Kim gets below Andy bellers out
"Get your goddamn ass out of there you fuckin squarehead
you wanna get killed?"
   We make an extra big pot of chocolate pudding at
the shelter that night, make Kim feel better.

   Surge Milkers: "This man had a good little brown
heifer that gave lots of milk, and one morning he put the
milker on her and went back inside and fell asleep
and slept an hour. And that little heifer had
mastitis in two days."

— — — —

Hitching south   ca. 21 Sept

        Down from Skykomish, evening light,
back of a convertible wind whipping the blanket
clear sky darkening the road winding along the river
willow and alder on the bank, a flat stretch of
green field; fir-covered hills beyond, dark
new barns and old barns—silvery shake barns—
        the new barns with tall round roofs.

92

— — — —

In Berkeley: 1 October 53

    "I am here to handle some of the preliminary
            arrangements fot the Apocalypse.
    Sand in pockets, sand in hair,
    Cigarettes that fell in seawater
    Set out to dry in the sun.
    Swimming in out of the way places
    In very cold water, creek or surf
    Is a great pleasure."
Under the Canary Island Pine
zazen and eating lunch. We are all immortals
            & the ground is damp.

Spring Sesshin at Shokoku-ji

Shokoku Temple is in northern Kyoto, on level ground, with a Christian college just south of it and many blocks of crowded little houses and stone-edged dirt roads north. It is the mother-temple of many branch temples scattered throughout Japan, and one of the several great temple-systems of the Rinzai Sect of Zen. Shokoku-ji is actually a compound: behind the big wood gate and tile-topped crumbling old mud walls are a number of temples each with its own gate and walls, gardens, and acres of wild bamboo grove. In the center of the compound is the soaring double-gabled Lecture Hall, silent and airy, an enormous dragon painted on the high ceiling, his eye burning down on the very center of the cut-slate floor. Except at infrequent rituals the hall is unused, and the gold-gilt Buddha sits on its high platform at the rear untroubled by drums and chanting. In front of the Lecture Hall is a long grove of fine young pines and a large square lotus-pond. To the east is a wooden belltower and the unpretentious gate of the Sodo, the training school for Zen monks, or Unsui.[1] They will become priests of Shokoku-ji temples. A few,

---

1 Unsui. The term is literally "cloud, water"—taken from a line of an old Chinese poem, "To drift like clouds and flow like water." It is strictly a Zen term. The Japanese word for Buddhist monks and priests of all sects is bozu (bonze). One takes no formal vows upon becoming an Unsui, although the head is shaved and a long Chinese-style robe called koromo is worn within Sodo walls. Unsui are free to quit the Zen community at any time. During the six months of the year in which the Sodo is in session (spring and fall) they eat no meat, but during the summer and winter off-periods they eat, drink and wear what they will. After becoming temple priests (Osho, Chinese Ho-shang), the great majority of Zen monks marry and raise families. The present generation of young Unsui is largely from temple families.

after years of zazen (meditation), koan study,[2] and final mastery of the Avatamsaka (Kegon) philosophy, become Roshi[3] (Zen Masters), qualified to head Sodos, teach lay groups, or do what they will. Laymen are also permitted to join the Unsui in evening Zendo (meditation hall) sessions, and some, like the Unsui, are given a koan by the Roshi and receive regular sanzen—the fierce face-to-face moment where you spit forth truth or perish—from him. Thus being driven, through time and much zazen, to the very end of the problem.

In the routine of Sodo life, there are special weeks during the year in which gardening, carpentry, reading and such, are suspended, and the time given over almost entirely to zazen. During these weeks, called sesshin, "concentrating the mind"—sanzen is received two to four times a day and hours of zazen in the Zendo are much extended. Laymen who will observe the customs of Sodo life and are able to sit still are allowed to join in the sesshin. At Shokoku-ji, the spring sesshin is held the first week of May.

The sesshin starts in the evening. The participants circle in single file into the mat-floored Central Hall of the Sodo and sit in a double row in dim light. The Roshi silently enters, sits at the head, and everyone drinks tea, each fishing his own teacup out of the deep-sleeved black robe. Then the Jikijitsu—head Unsui of the Zendo (a position which revolves among the older men, changing

2 Koans are usually short anecdotes concerning the incomprehensible and illogical behavior and language of certain key Chinese Zen Masters of the T'ang Dynasty. The koan assigned to the student is the subject of his meditation, and his understanding of it is the subject of sanzen, an interview with the Zen Master. Very advanced students are also required to relate koan-understanding to the intellectual concepts of Buddhist philosophy.

3 Roshi. Literally, "old master"—Chinese Lao-shih. A Roshi is not simply a person who "understands" Zen, but specifically a person who has received the seal of approval from his own Zen Master and is his "Dharma heir." A person may comprehend Zen to the point that his Roshi will say he has no more to teach him, but if the Roshi does not feel the student is intellectually and scholastically equipped to transmit Zen as well, he will not permit him to be his heir. Most Roshi are Zen monks, but laymen and women have also achieved this title.

every six months)—reads in formal voice the rules of Zendo and sesshin, written in Sung Dynasty Sino-Japanese. The Roshi says you all must work very hard; all bow and go out, returning to the Zendo for short meditation and early sleep.

At three a.m. the Fusu (another older Zenbo who is in charge of finances and meeting people) appears in the Zendo ringing a hand-bell. Lights go on—ten-watt things tacked under the beams of a building lit for centuries by oil lamps—and everyone wordlessly and swiftly rolls up his single quilt and stuffs it in a small cupboard at the rear of his mat, leaps off the raised platform that rings the hall, to the stone floor, and scuffs out in straw sandals to dash icy water on the face from a stone bowl. They come back quickly and sit crosslegged on their zazen cushions, on the same mat used for sleeping. The Jikijitsu stalks in and sits at his place, lighting a stick of incense and beginning the day with the rifleshot crack of a pair of hardwood blocks whacked together and a ding on a small bronze bell. Several minutes of silence, and another whack is heard from the Central Hall. Standing up and slipping on the sandals, the group files out of the Zendo, trailing the Jikijitsu—who hits his bell as he walks—and goes down the roofed stone path, fifty yards long, that joins the Zendo and the Central Hall. Forming two lines and sitting on the mats, they begin to chant sutras. The choppy Sino-Japanese words follow the rhythm of a fish-shaped wooden drum and a deep-throated bell. They roar loud and chant fast. The Roshi enters and between the two lines makes deep bows to the Buddha-image before him, lights incense, and retires. The hard-thumping drum and sutra-songs last an hour, then suddenly stop and all return to the Zendo. Each man standing before his place, they chant the *Prajña-paramita-hridaya Sutra,* the Jikijitsu going so fast now no one can follow him. Then hoisting themselves onto the mats, they meditate. After half an hour a harsh bell-clang is heard from the Roshi's quarters. The Jikijitsu bellows "Getout" and the Zenbos dash out racing, feet slapping the cold stones and robes flying, to kneel in line whatever order they make it before the sanzen room. A ring of the bell marks each new entrance before the

Roshi. All one hears from outside is an occasional growl and some-times the whack of a stick. The men return singly and subdued from sanzen to their places.

Not all return. Some go to the kitchen, to light brushwood fires in the brick stoves and cook rice in giant black pots. When they are ready they signal with a clack of wood blocks, and those in the Ze-ndo answer by a ring on the bell. Carrying little nested sets of bowls and extra-large chopsticks, they come down the covered walk. It is getting light, and at this time of year the azalea are blooming. The moss-floored garden on both sides of the walk is thick with them, banks under pine and maple, white flowers glowing through mist. Even the meal, nothing but salty radish pickles and thin rice gruel, is begun and ended by whacks of wood and chanting of short verses. After breakfast the Zenbos scatter: some to wash pots, others to mop the long wood verandas of the central hall and sweep and mop the Roshi's rooms or rake leaves and paths in the garden. The younger Unsui and the outsiders dust, sweep, and mop the Zendo.

The Shokoku-ji Zendo is one of the largest and finest in Japan. It is on a raised terrace of stone and encircled by a stone walk. Outside a long overhang roof and dark unpainted wood—inside round log posts set on granite footings—it is always cool and dark and very still. The floor is square slate laid diagonal. The raised wood plat-form that runs around the edge has mats for forty men. Sitting in a three-walled box that hangs from the center of the ceiling, like an overhead-crane operator, is a lifesize wood statue of the Buddha's disciple Kasyapa, his eyes real and piercing anyone who enters the main door. In an attached room to the rear of the Zendo is a shrine to the founder of Shokoku-ji, his statue in wood, eyes peering out of a dark alcove.

By seven a.m. the routine chores are done and the Jikijitsu in-vites those cleaning up the Zendo into his room for tea. The Jiki-jitsu and the Fusu both have private quarters, the Fusu lodging in the Central Hall and the Jikijitsu in a small building adjoining the Zendo. The chill is leaving the air, and he slides open the paper screens, opening a wall of his room to the outside. Sitting on mats and drinking tea they relax and smoke and quietly kid a little, and the Jikijitsu—a tigerish terror during the zazen sessions—is very gentle. "You'll be a Roshi one of these days" a medical student staying the week said to him. "Not me, I can't grasp koans," he laughs, rubbing his shaved head where the Roshi has knocked him recently. Then they talk of work to be done around the Sodo. During sesshin periods work is kept to a minimum, but some must be done. Taking off robes and putting on ragged old dungarees everyone spreads out, some to the endless task of weeding grass from the moss garden, others to the vegetable plots. The Jikijitsu takes a big mattock and heads for the bamboo-grove to chop out a few bamboo shoots for the kitchen. Nobody works very hard, and several times during the morning they find a warm place in the sun and smoke.

At ten-thirty they quit work and straggle to the kitchen for lunch, the main meal. Miso-soup full of vegetables, plenty of rice and several sorts of pickles. The crunch of bicycles and shouts of children playing around the belltower can be heard just beyond the wall. After lunch the laymen and younger Unsui return to the Zendo. More experienced men have the greater responsibilities of running the Sodo, and they keep busy at accounts, shopping and looking after the needs of the Roshi. Afternoon sitting in the Zendo is informal—newcomers take plenty of time getting comfortable, and occasionally go out to walk and smoke a bit. Conversation is not actually forbidden, but no one wants to talk.

Shortly before three, things tighten up and the Jikijitsu comes in. When everyone is gathered, and a bell heard from the Central Hall, they march out for afternoon sutra-chanting. The sutras recited vary from day to day, and as the leader announces new titles some men produce books from their sleeves to read by, for not all have yet memorized them completely. Returning to the Zendo, they again recite the *Prajña-paramita-hridaya Sutra,* and the Jikijitsu chants a piece alone, his voice filling the hall, head tilted up to the statue of Kasyapa, hand cupped to his mouth as though calling across miles.

After sitting a few minutes the signal is heard for evening meal, and all file into the kitchen, stand, chant, sit, and lay out their bowls. No one speaks. Food is served with a gesture of "giving," and one stops the server with a gesture of "enough." At the end of the meal—rice and pickles—a pot of hot water is passed and each man pours some into his bowls, swashes it around and drinks it, wipes out his bowls with a little cloth. Then they are nested again, wrapped in their cover, and everyone stands and leaves.

It is dusk and the Zendo is getting dark inside. All the Zenbos begin to assemble now, some with their cushions tucked under arm, each bowing before Kasyapa as he enters. Each man, right hand held up before the chest flat like a knife and cutting the air, walks straight to his place, bows toward the center of the room, arranges the cushions, and assumes the crosslegged "half-lotus" posture. Others arrive too—teachers, several college professors and half a dozen university students wearing the black uniforms that serve for classrooms, bars and temples equally well—being all they own. Some enter uncertainly and bow with hesitation, afraid of making mistakes, curious to try zazen and overwhelmed by the historical weight of Zen, something very "Japanese" and very "high class." One student, most threadbare of all, had a head shaved like an Unsui and entered with knowledge and precision every night, sitting perfectly still on his cushions and acknowledging no one. By seven-thirty the hall is half full—a sizable number of people for present-day Zen sessions—and the great bell in the belltower booms. As it booms, the man ringing it, swinging a long wood-beam ram, sings out a sutra over the shops and homes of the neighborhood. When he has finished, the faint lights in the Zendo go on and evening zazen has begun.

The Jikijitsu sits at the head of the hall, marking the half-hour periods with wood clackers and bell. He keeps a stick of incense burning beside him, atop a small wood box that says "not yet" on it in Chinese. At the end of the first half-hour he claps the blocks once and grunts "kinhin." This is "walking zazen," and the group stands—the Unsui tying up sleeves and tucking up robes—and at another signal they start marching single file around the inside of the hall. They walk fast and unconsciously in step, the Jikijitsu leading with a long samurai stride. They circle and circle, through shadow and under the light, ducking below Kasyapa's roost, until suddenly the Jikijitsu claps his blocks and yells "Getout!"—the circle broken and everyone dashing for the door. Night sanzen. Through the next twenty minutes they return to resume meditation—not preparing an answer now, but considering the Roshi's response.

Zazen is a very tight thing. The whole room feels it. The Jikijitsu gets up, grasps a long flat stick and begins to slowly prowl the hall, stick on shoulder, walking before the rows of sitting men, each motionless with eyes half-closed and looking straight ahead downward. An inexperienced man sitting out of balance will be lightly tapped and prodded into easier posture. An Unsui sitting poorly will be without warning roughly knocked off his cushions. He gets up and sits down again. Nothing is said. Anyone showing signs of drowsiness will feel a light tap of the stick on the shoulder. He and the Jikijitsu then bow to each other, and the man leans forward to receive four blows on each side of his back. These are not particularly painful—though the loud whack of them can be terrifying to a newcomer—and serve to wake one well. One's legs may hurt during long sitting, but there is no relief until the Jikijitsu rings his bell. The mind must simply be placed elsewhere. At the end of an hour the bell does ring and the second kinhin begins—a welcome twenty minutes of silent rhythmic walking. The walking ends abruptly and anyone not seated and settled when the Jikijitsu whips around the hall is knocked off his cushion. Zen aims at freedom but its practice is disciplined.

Several Unsui slip out during kinhin. At ten they return—they can be heard coming, running full speed down the walk. They enter carrying big trays of hot noodles, udon, in large lacquer bowls. They bow to the Jikijitsu and circle the room setting a bowl before each man; giving two or even three bowls to those who want them. Each man bows, takes up chopsticks, and eats the noodles as fast as he can. Zenbos are famous for fast noodle-eating and no one wants to be last done. As the empty bowls are set down they are gathered up and one server follows, wiping the beam that fronts the mats with a rag, at a run. At the door the servers stop and bow to the group. It bows in return. Then one server announces the person—usually a friend or patron of the Sodo—who footed the bill for the sesshin noodles that night. The group bows again. Meditation is resumed. At ten-thirty there is another rest period and men gather to smoke and chat a little in back. "Are there really some Americans interested in Zen?" they ask with astonishment—for their own countrymen pay them scant attention.

At eleven bells ring and wood clacks, and final sutras are chanted. The hall is suddenly filled with huge voices. The evening visitors take their cushions and leave, each bowing to the Jikijitsu and Kasyapa as he goes. The others flip themselves into their sleeping quilts immediately and lie dead still. The Jikijitsu pads once around, says, "Take counsel of your pillow," and walks out. The hall goes black. But this is not the end, for as soon as the lights go out, everyone gets up again and takes his sitting cushion, slips outside, and practices zazen alone wherever he likes for another two hours. The next day begins at three a.m.

This is the daily schedule of the sesshin. On several mornings during the week, the Roshi gives a lecture (teisho) based on some anecdote in the Zen textbooks—usually from *Mumonkan* or *Heki-ganroku*. As the group sits in the Central Hall awaiting his entrance, one Zenbo stands twirling a stick around the edge-tacks of a big drum, filling the air with a deep reverberation. The Roshi sits crosslegged on a very high chair, receives a cup of tea, and delivers lectures that might drive some mad—for he tells these poor souls beating their brains out night after night that "the Perfect Way is without difficulty" and he means it and they know he's right.

In the middle of the week everyone gets a bath and a new head-shave. There is a Zen saying that "while studying koans you should not relax even in the bath," but this one is never heeded. The bathhouse contains two deep iron tubs, heated by brushwood fires stoked below from outside. The blue smoke and sweet smell of crackling hinoki and sugi twigs, stuffed in by a fire-tender, and the men taking a long time and getting really clean. Even in the bathhouse you bow—to a small shrine high on the wall—both before and after bathing. The Jikijitsu whets up his razor and shaves heads, but shaves his own alone and without mirror. He never nicks himself any more.

On the day after bath they go begging (takuhatsu). It rained this day, but putting on oiled-paper slickers over their robes and wearing straw sandals they splashed out. The face of the begging Zenbo can scarcely be seen, for he wears a deep bowl-shaped woven straw hat. They walk slowly, paced far apart, making a weird wailing sound as they go, never stopping. Sometimes they walk for miles, crisscrossing the little lanes and streets of Kyoto. They came back soaked, chanting a sutra as they entered the Sodo gate, and added up a meager take. The rain sluiced down all that afternoon, making a green twilight inside the Zendo and a rush of sound.

The next morning during tea with the Jikijitsu, a college professor who rents rooms in one of the Sodo buildings came in and talked of koans. "When you understand Zen, you know that the tree is really *there*."—The only time anyone said anything of Zen philosophy or experience the whole week. Zenbos never discuss koans or sanzen experience with each other.

The sesshin ends at dawn on the eighth day. All who have participated gather in the Jikijitsu's room and drink powdered green tea and eat cakes. They talk easily, it's over. The Jikijitsu, who has whacked or knocked them all during the week, is their great friend now—compassion takes many forms.

Passage To More Than India

> "It will be a revival, in higher form, of the liberty,
> equality, and fraternity of the ancient gentes."
> —LEWIS HENRY MORGAN

The Tribe

The celebrated human Be-In in San Francisco, January of 1967, was called "A Gathering of the Tribes." The two posters: one based on a photograph of a Shaivite sadhu with his long matted hair, ashes and beard; the other based on an old etching of a Plains Indian approaching a powwow on his horse—the carbine that had been cradled in his left arm replaced by a guitar. The Indians, and the Indian. The tribes were Berkeley, North Beach, Big Sur, Marin County, Los Angeles, and the host, Haight-Ashbury. Outriders were present from New York, London and Amsterdam. Out on the polo field that day the splendidly clad ab/originals often fell into clusters, with children, a few even under banners. These were the clans.

Large old houses are rented communally by a group, occupied by couples and singles (or whatever combinations) and their children. In some cases, especially in the rock-and-roll business and with light-show groups, they are all working together on the same creative job. They might even be a legal corporation. Some are subsistence farmers out in the country, some are contractors and carpenters in small coast towns. One girl can stay home and look after all the children while the other girls hold jobs. They will all be cooking and eating together and they may well be brown-rice vegetarians. There might not be much alcohol or tobacco around the house, but there will certainly be a stash of marijuana and

103

probably some LSD. If the group has been together for some time it may be known by some informal name, magical and natural. These house-holds provide centers in the city and also out in the country for loners and rangers; gathering places for the scattered smaller hip families and havens for the questing adolescent children of the neighborhood. The clan sachems will sometimes gather to talk about larger issues—police or sheriff department harassments, busts, anti-Vietnam projects, dances and gatherings.

All this is known fact. The number of committed total tribesmen is not so great, but there is a large population of crypto-members who move through many walks of life undetected and only put on their beads and feathers for special occasions. Some are in the academies, others in the legal or psychiatric profession—very useful friends indeed. The number of people who use marijuana regularly and have experienced LSD is (considering it's all illegal) staggering. The impact of all this on the cultural and imaginative life of the nation—even the politics—is enormous

And yet, there's nothing very new about it, in spite of young hippies just in from the suburbs for whom the "beat generation" is a kalpa away. For several centuries now Western Man has been ponderously preparing himself for a new look at the inner world and the spiritual realms. Even in the centers of nineteenth-century materialism there were dedicated seekers—some within Christianity, some in the arts, some within the occult circles. Witness William Butler Yeats. My own opinion is that we are now experiencing a surfacing (in a specifically "American" incarnation) of the Great Subculture which goes back as far perhaps as the late Paleolithic.

This subculture of illuminati has been a powerful undercurrent in all higher civilizations. In China it manifested as Taoism, not only Lao-tzu but the later Yellow Turban revolt and medieval Taoist secret societies; and the Zen Buddhists up till early Sung. Within Islam the Sufis; in India the various threads converged to produce Tantrism. In the West it has been represented largely by a string of heresies starting with the Gnostics, and on the folk level by "witchcraft."

Buddhist Tantrism, or Vajrayana as it's also known, is probably the finest and most modern statement of this ancient shamanistic-yogic-gnostic-socioeconomic view: that mankind's mother is Nature and Nature should be tenderly respected; that man's life and destiny is growth and enlightenment in self-disciplined freedom; that the divine has been made flesh and that flesh is divine; that we not only should but *do* love one another. This view has been harshly suppressed in the past as threatening to both Church and State. Today, on the contrary, these values seem almost biologically essential to the survival of humanity.

The Family

Lewis Henry Morgan (d. 1881) was a New York lawyer. He was asked by his club to reorganize it "after the pattern of the Iroquois confederacy." His research converted him into a defender of tribal rights and started him on his career as an amateur anthropologist. His major contribution was broad theory of social evolution which is still useful. Morgan's *Ancient Society* inspired Engels to write *Origins of the Family, Private Property and the State* (1884, and still in print in both Russia and China), in which the relations between the rights of women, sexuality and the family, and attitudes toward property and power are tentatively explored. The pivot is the revolutionary implications of the custom of matrilineal descent, which Engels learned from Morgan; the Iroquois are matrilineal.

A schematic history of the family:

Hunters and gatherers—a loose monogamy within communal clans usually reckoning descent in the female line, i.e., matrilineal.

Early agriculturalists—a tendency toward group and polyandrous marriage, continued matrilineal descent and smaller-sized clans.

Pastoral nomads—a tendency toward stricter monogamy and patrilineal descent; but much premarital sexual freedom.

Iron-Age agriculturalists—property begins to accumulate and the family system changes to monogamy or polygyny with patrilineal descent. Concern with the legitimacy of heirs.

Civilization so far has implied a patriarchal patrilineal family. Any other system allows too much creative sexual energy to be released into channels which are "unproductive." In the West, the clan, or gens, disappeared gradually, and social organization was ultimately replaced by political organization, within which separate male-oriented families compete: the modern state.

Engels' Marxian classic implies that the revolution cannot be completely achieved in merely political terms. Monogamy and patrilineal descent may well be great obstructions to the inner changes required for a people to truly live by "communism." Marxists after Engels let these questions lie. Russia and China today are among the world's staunchest supporters of monogamous, sexually turned-off families. Yet Engels' insights were not entirely ignored. The Anarcho-Syndicalists showed a sense for experimental social reorganization. American anarchists and the I.W.W. lived a kind of communalism, with some lovely stories handed down of free love—their slogan was more than just words: "Forming the new society within the shell of the old." San Francisco poets and gurus were attending meetings of the "Anarchist Circle"—old Italians and Finns—in the 1940's.

The Redskins

In many American Indian cultures it is obligatory for every member to get out of the society, out of the human nexus, and "out of his head," at least once in his life. He returns from his solitary vision quest with a secret name, a protective animal spirit, a secret song. It is his "power." The culture honors the man who has visited other realms.

Peyote, the mushroom, morning-glory seeds and Jimson-weed are some of the best-known herbal aids used by Indian cultures to assist in the quest. Most tribes apparently achieved these results simply through yogic-type disciplines: including sweat-baths, hours of dancing, fasting and total isolation. After the decline of the apocalyptic fervor of Wovoka's Ghost Dance religion (a pan-Indian movement of the 1880's and 1890's which believed that if all the Indians would dance the Ghost Dance with their Ghost shirts on, the buffalo would rise from the ground, trample the white men to death in their dreams, and all the dead game would return; America would be restored to the Indians), the peyote cult spread and established itself in most of the western American tribes. Although the peyote religion conflicts with pre-existing tribal religions in a few cases (notably with the Pueblo), there is no doubt that the cult has been a positive force, helping the Indians maintain a reverence for their traditions and land through their period of greatest weakness—which is now over. European scholars were investigating peyote in the twenties. It is even rumored that Dr. Carl Jung was experimenting with peyote then. A small band of white peyote users emerged, and peyote was easily available in San Francisco by the late 1940's. In Europe some researchers on these alkaloid compounds were beginning to synthesize them. There is a karmic connection between the peyote cult of the Indians and the discovery of lysergic acid in Switzerland.

Peyote and acid have a curious way of tuning some people in to the local soil. The strains and stresses deep beneath one in the rock, the flow and fabric of wildlife around, the human history of Indians on this continent. Older powers become evident: west of the Rockies, the ancient creator-trickster, Coyote. Jaime de Angulo, a now-legendary departed Spanish shaman and anthropologist, was an authentic Coyote-medium. One of the most revelant poetry magazines is called *Coyote's Journal*. For many, the invisible presence of the Indian, and the heartbreaking beauty of America work without fasting or herbs. We make these contacts simply by walking the Sierra or Mohave, learning the old edibles, singing and watching.

The Jewel in the Lotus

At the Congress of World Religions in Chicago in the 1890's, two of the most striking figures were Swami Vivekananda (Shri

Ramakrishna's disciples) and Shaku Soyen, the Zen Master and Abbot of Engaku-ji, representing Japanese Rinzai Zen. Shaku Soyen's interpreter was a college student named Teitaro Suzuki. The Ramakrishna-Vivekananda line produced scores of books and established Vedanta centers all through the Western world. A small band of Zen monks under Shaku Sokatsu (disciple of Shaku Soyen) was raising strawberries in Hayward, California, in 1907. Shigetsu Sasaki, later to be known as the Zen Master Sokei-an, was roaming the timberlands of the Pacific Northwest just before World War I, and living on a Puget Sound Island with Indians for neighbors. D. T. Suzuki's books are to be found today in the libraries of biochemists and on stone ledges under laurel trees in the open-air camps of Big Sur gypsies.

A Californian named Walter Y. Evans-Wentz, who sensed that the mountains on his family's vast grazing lands really did have spirits in them, went to Oxford to study the Celtic belief in fairies and then to Sikkim to study Vajrayana under a lama. His best-known book is *The Tibetan Book of the Dead.*

Those who do not have the money or time to go to India or Japan, but who think a great deal about the wisdom traditions, have remarkable results when they take LSD. The *Bhagavad-Gita,* the Hindu mythologies, *The Serpent Power,* the *Lankavatara-sūtra,* the *Upanishads,* the *Hevajra-tantra,* the *Mahanirvana-tantra*—to name a few texts—become, they say, finally clear to them. They often feel they must radically reorganize their lives to harmonize with such insights.

In several American cities traditional meditation halls of both Rinzai and Soto Zen are flourishing. Many of the newcomers turned to traditional meditation after initial acid experience. The two types of experience seem to inform each other.

The Heretics

"When Adam delved and Eve span,
    Who was then a gentleman?"

The memories of a Golden Age—the Garden of Eden—the Age of the Yellow Ancestor—were genuine expressions of civilization and its discontents. Harking back to societies where women and men were more free with each other; where there was more singing and dancing; where there were no serfs and priests and kings.

Projected into future time in Christian culture, this dream of the Millennium became the soil of many heresies. It is a dream handed down right to our own time—of ecological balance, class-less society, social and economic freedom. It is actually one of the possible futures open to us. To those who stubbornly argue "it's against human nature," we can only patiently reply that you must know your own nature before you can say this. Those who have gone into their own natures deeply have, for several thousand years now, been reporting that we have nothing to fear if we are willing to train ourselves, to open up, explore and grow.

One of the most significant medieval heresies was the Brother-hood of the Free Spirit, of which Hieronymus Bosch was probably a member. The Brotherhood believed that God was immanent in everything, and that once one had experienced this God-presence in himself he became a Free Spirit; he was again living in the Garden of Eden. The brothers and sisters held their meetings naked, and practiced much sharing. They "confounded clerics with the subtlety of their arguments." It was complained that "they have no uniform ... sometimes they dress in a costly and dissolute fashion, sometimes most miserably, all according to time and place." The Free Spirits had communal houses in secret all through Germany and the Lowlands, and wandered freely among them. Their main supporters were the well-organized and affluent weavers.

When brought before the Inquisition they were not charged with witchcraft, but with believing that man was divine, and with making love too freely, with orgies. Thousands were burned. There are some who have as much hostility to the adepts of the subculture today. This may be caused not so much by the outlandish clothes and dope, as by the nutty insistence on "love." The West and Christian culture on one level deeply wants love to win—and having

109

decided (after several sad tries) that love can't, people who still say it will are like ghosts from an old dream.

Love begins with the family and its network of erotic and responsible relationships. A slight alteration of family structure will project a different love-and-property outlook through a whole culture ... thus the communism and free love of the Christian heresies. This is a real razor's edge. Shall the lion lie down with the lamb? And make love even? The Garden of Eden.

White Indians

The modern American family is the smallest and most barren family that has ever existed. Each newly-married couple moves to a new house or apartment—no uncles or grandmothers come to live with them. There are seldom more than two or three children. The children live with their peers and leave home early. Many have never had the least sense of family.

I remember sitting down to Christmas dinner eighteen years ago in a communal house in Portland, Oregon, with about twelve others my own age, all of whom had no place they wished to go home to. That house was my first discovery of harmony and community with fellow beings. This has been the experience of hundreds of thousands of men and women all over America since the end of World War II. Hence the talk about the growth of a "new society." But more; these gatherings have been people spending time with each other—talking, delving, making love. Because of the sheer amount of time "wasted" together (without TV) they know each other better than most Americans know their family. Add to this the mind-opening and personality-revealing effects of grass and acid, and it becomes possible to predict the emergence of groups who live by mutual illumination—have seen themselves as of one mind and one flesh—the "single eye" of the heretical English Ranters; The meaning of sahajiya, "born together"—the name of the latest flower of the Tantric community tradition in Bengal.

Industrial society indeed appears to be finished. Many of us are, again, hunters and gathers. Poets, musicians, nomadic engineers and scholars; fact-diggers, searchers and re-searchers scoring in rich foundation territory. Horse-traders in lore and magic. The super hunting-bands of mercenaries like Rand or CIA may in some ways belong to the future, if they can be transformed by the ecological conscience, or acid, to which they are very vulnerable. A few of us are literally hunters and gatherers, playfully studying the old techniques of acorn flour, seaweed-gathering, yucca-fiber, rabbit snaring and bow hunting. The densest Indian population in pre-Columbian America north of Mexico was in Marin, Sonoma and Napa Countries, California.

And finally, to go back to Morgan and Engels, sexual mores and the family are changing in the same direction. Rather than the "breakdown of the family" we should see this as the transition to a new form of family. In the near future, I think it likely that the freedom of women and the tribal spirit will make it possible for us to formalize our marriage relationships in any way we please—as groups, or polygynously or polyandrously, as well as monogamously. I use the word "formalize" only in the sense of make public and open the relationships, and to sacramentalize them; to see family as part of the divine ecology. Because it is simpler, more natural, and breaks up tendencies toward property accumulation by individual families, matrilineal descent seems ultimately indicated. Such families already exist. Their children are different in personality structure and outlook from anybody in the history of Western culture since the destruction of Knossos.

The American Indian is the vengeful ghost lurking in the back of the troubled American mind. Which is why we lash out with such ferocity and passion, so muddied a heart, at the black-haired young peasants and soldiers who are the "Viet Cong." That ghost will claim the next generation as its own. When this has happened, citizens of the USA will at last begin to be Americans, truly at home on the continent, in love with their land. The chorus of a Cheyenne Indian Ghost dance song—"hi-niswa' vita'ki'ni"—"We shall live again."

"Passage to more than India!
Are thy wings plumed indeed for such far flights?
O soul, voyagest thou indeed on voyages like those?"

Poetry and the Primitive

Notes on Poetry as an Ecological Survival Technique

Bilateral Symmetry

"Poetry" as the skilled and inspired use of the voice and language to embody rare and powerful states of mind that are in immediate origin personal to the singer, but at deep levels common to all who listen. "Primitive" as those societies which have remained non-literate and non-political while necessarily exploring and developing in directions that civilized societies have tended to ignore. Having fewer tools, no concern with history, a living oral tradition rather than an accumulated library, no overriding social goals, and considerable freedom of sexual and inner life, such people live vastly in the present. Their daily reality is a fabric of friends and family, the field of feeling and energy that one's own body is, the earth they stand on and the wind that wraps around it; and various areas of consciousness.

At this point some might be tempted to say that the primitive's real life is no different from anybody else's. I think this is not so. To live in the "mythological present" in close relation to nature and in basic but disciplined body/mind states suggests a wider-ranging imagination and a closer subjective knowledge of one's own physical properties than is usually available to men living (as they themselves describe it) impotently and inadequately in "history"—their

113

mind-content programmed, and their caressing of nature compli-
cated by the extensions and abstractions which elaborate tools are.
A hand pushing a button may wield great power, but that hand
will never learn what a hand can do. Unused capacities go sour.

Poetry must sing or speak from authentic experience. Of all the
streams of civilized tradition with roots in the paleolithic, poetry
is one of the few that can realistically claim an unchanged function
and a relevance which will outlast most of the activities that sur-
round us today. Poets, as few others, must live close to the world
that primitive men are in: the world, in its nakedness, which is
fundamental for all of us—birth, love, death; the sheer fact of be-
ing alive.

Music, dance, religion, and philosophy of course have archaic
roots—a shared origin with poetry. Religion has tended to become
the social justifier, a lackey to power, instead of the vehicle of hair-
raising liberating and healing realizations. Dance has mostly lost
its connection with ritual drama, the miming of animals, or tracing
the maze of the spiritual journey. Most music takes too many tools.
The poet can make it on his own voice and mother tongue, while
steering a course between crystal clouds of utterly incommunicable
non-verbal states—and the gleaming daggers and glittering nets
of language.

In one school of Mahayana Buddhism, they talk about the "Three
Mysteries." These are Body, Voice, and Mind. The things that are
what living *is* for us, in life. Poetry is the vehicle of the mystery of
voice. The universe, as they sometimes say, is a vast breathing body.

With artists, certain kinds of scientists, yogins, and poets, a kind
of mind-sense is not only surviving but modestly flourishing in the
twentieth century. Claude Lévi-Strauss (*The Savage Mind*) sees no
problem in the continuity: "... it is neither the mind of savages
nor that of primitive or archaic humanity, but rather mind in its
untamed state as distinct from mind cultivated or domesticated for
yielding a return ... We are better able to understand today that it
is possible for the two to coexist and interpenetrate in the same way
that (in theory at least) it is possible for natural species, of which

114

some are in their savage state and others transformed by agriculture and domestication, to coexist and cross ... whether one deplores or rejoices in the fact, there are still zones in which savage thought, like savage species, is relatively protected. This is the case of art, to which our civilization accords the status of a national park."

Making Love with Animals

By civilized times, hunting was a sport of kings. The early Chinese emperors had vast fenced hunting reserves; peasants were not allowed to shoot deer. Millennia of experience, the proud knowledge of hunting magic—animal habits—and the skills of wild plant and herb gathering were all but scrubbed away. Much has been said about the frontier in American history, but overlooking perhaps some key points: the American confrontation with a vast wild ecology, an earthly paradise of grass, water, and game—was mind-shaking. Americans lived next to vigorous primitives whom they could not help but respect and even envy, for three hundred years. Finally, as ordinary men supporting their families, they often hunted for food. Although marginal peasants in Europe and Asia did remain part-time hunters at the bottom of the social scale, these Americans were the vanguard of an expanding culture. For Americans, "nature" means wilderness, the untamed realm of total freedom—not brutish and nasty, but beautiful and terrible. Something is always eating at the American heart like acid: it is the knowledge of what we have done to our continent, and to the American Indian.

Other civilizations have done the same, but at a pace too slow to be remembered. One finds evidence in T'ang and Sung poetry that the barren hills of central and northern China were once richly forested. The Far Eastern love of nature has become fear of nature: gardens and pine trees are tormented and controlled. Chinese nature poets were too often retired bureaucrats living on two or three acres of trees trimmed by hired gardeners. The professional nature-aesthetes of modern Japan, tea-teachers and flower-arrangers, are amazed to hear that only a century ago dozens of species of birds passed through Kyoto where today only swallows and sparrows can be seen; and the aesthetes can scarcely distinguish those. "Wild" in the Far East means uncontrollable, objectionable, crude, sexually unrestrained, violent; actually ritually polluting. China cast off mythology, which means its own dreams, with hairy cocks and gaping pudenda, millennia ago; and modern Japanese families participating in an "economic miracle" can have daughters in college who are not sure which hole babies come out of. One of the most remarkable intuitions in Western thought was Rousseau's Noble Savage: the idea that perhaps civilization has something to learn from the primitive.

Man is a beautiful animal. We know this because other animals admire us and love us. Almost all animals are beautiful and paleolithic hunters were deeply moved by it. To hunt means to use your body and senses to the fullest: to strain your consciousness to feel what the deer are thinking today, this moment; to sit still and let your self go into the birds and wind while waiting by a game trail. Hunting magic is designed to bring the game to you—the creature who has heard your song, witnessed your sincerity, and out of compassion comes within your range. Hunting magic is not only aimed at bringing beasts to their death, but to assist in their birth—to promote their fertility. Thus the great Iberian cave paintings are not of hunting alone—but of animals mating and giving birth. A Spanish farmer who saw some reproductions from Altamira is reported to have said, "How beautifully this cow gives birth to a calf!" Breuil has said, "The religion of those days did *not* elevate the animal to the position of a god ... but it was *humbly entreated* to be fertile." A Haida incantation goes:

> "The Great One coming up against the current
>   begins thinking of it
> The Great One coming putting gravel in his mouth
>   thinks of it
> You look at it with white stone eyes—
>   Great Eater begins thinking of it."

People of primitive cultures appreciate animals as other people off on various trips. Snakes move without limbs, and are like free penises. Birds fly, sing, and dance; they gather food for their babies; they disappear for months and then come back. Fish can breathe water and are brilliant colors. Mammals are like us, they fuck and give birth to babies while panting and purring; their young suck their mothers' breasts; they know terror and delight, they play.

Lévi-Strauss quotes Swanton's report on the Chickasaw, the tribe's own amusing game of seeing the different clans as acting out the lives of their totemic emblems: "The Raccoon people were said to live on fish and wild fruit, those of the Puma lived in the mountains, avoided water of which they were very frightened and lived principally on game. The Wild Cat clan slept in the daytime and hunted at night, for they had keen eyes; they were indifferent to women. Members of the Bird clan were up before daybreak: 'They were like real birds in that they would not bother anybody ... the people of this clan have different sorts of minds, just as there are different species of birds.' They were said to live well, to be polygamous, disinclined to work, and prolific ... the inhabitants of the 'bending-post-oak' house group lived in the woods ... the High Corncrib house people were respected in spite of their arrogance: they were good gardeners, very industrious but poor hunters; they bartered their maize for game. They were said to be truthful and stubborn, and skilled at forecasting the weather. As for the Redskunk house group: they lived in dugouts underground."

We all know what primitive cultures don't have. What they *do* have is this knowledge of connection and responsibility which amounts to a spiritual ascesis for the whole community. Monks of Christianity or Buddhism, "leaving the world" (which means the games of society) are trying, in a decadent way, to achieve what whole primitive communities—men, women, and children—live by daily; and with more wholeness. The Shaman-poet is simply the man whose mind reaches easily out into all manners of shapes and other lives, and gives song to dreams. Poets have carried this function forward all through civilized times: poets don't sing about society, they sing about nature—even if the closest they ever get to nature is their lady's queynt. Class-structured civilized society is a kind of mass ego. To transcend the ego is to go beyond society as well. "Beyond" there lies, inwardly, the unconscious. Outwardly, the equivalent of the unconscious is the wilderness: both of these terms meet, one step even farther on, as *one*.

One religious tradition of this communion with nature which has survived into historic Western times is what has been called Witchcraft. The antlered and pelted figure painted on the cave wall of Trois Fréres, a shaman-dancer-poet, is a prototype of both Shiva and the Devil.

Animal marriages (and supernatural marriages) are a common motif of folklore the world around. A recent article by Lynn White puts the blame for the present ecological crisis on the Judaeo-Christian tradition—animals don't have souls and can't be saved; nature is merely a ground for us to exploit while working out our drama of free will and salvation under the watch of Jehovah. The Devil? "The Deivill apeired vnto her in the liknes of ane prettie boy in grein clothes ... and at that tyme the Deivil gaive hir his markis; and went away from her in the liknes of ane blak dowg." "He wold haw carnall dealling with ws in the shap of a deir, or in any vther shap, now and then, somtyme he vold be lyk a stirk, a bull, a deir, a rae, or a dowg, etc, and haw dealling with us."

The archaic and primitive ritual dramas, which acknowledged all the sides of human nature, including the destructive, demonic, and ambivalent, were liberating and harmonizing. Freud said *he* didn't discover the unconscious, poets had centuries before. The purpose of California Shamanism was "to heal disease and resist death, with a power acquired from dreams." An Arapaho dancer of the Ghost Dance came back from his trance to sing:

"I circle around, I circle around

The boundaries of the earth,
The boundaries of the earth

Wearing the long wing feathers as I fly
Wearing the long wing feathers as I fly."

The Voice as a Girl

"Everything was alive—the trees, grasses, and winds were dancing
with me, talking with me; I could understand the songs of the
birds." This ancient experience is not so much—in spite of later
commentators—"religious" as it is a pure perception of beauty. The
phenomenal world experienced at certain pitches is totally living,
exciting, mysterious, filling one with a trembling awe, leaving one
grateful and humble. The wonder of the mystery returns direct to
one's own senses and consciousness: inside and outside; the voice
breathes, "Ah!"

Breath is the outer world coming into one's body. With pulse—
the two always harmonizing—the source of our inward sense of
rhythm. Breath is spirit, "inspiration." Expiration, "voiced." makes
the signals by which the species connects. Certain emotions and
states occasionally seize the body, one becomes a whole tube of
air vibrating; all voice. In mantra chanting, the magic utterances,
built of seed-syllables such as OM and AYNG and AH, repeated
over and over, fold and curl on the breath until—when most weary
and bored—a new voice enters, a voice speaks through you clearer
and stronger than what you know of yourself; with a sureness and
melody of its own, singing out the inner song of the self, and of
the planet.

Poetry, it should not have to be said, is not writing or books.
Non-literate cultures with their traditional training methods of
hearing and reciting, carry thousands of poems—death, war, love,
dream, work, and spirit-power songs—through time. The voice of
inspiration as an "other" has long been known in the West as The
Muse. Widely speaking, the muse is anything other that touches
you and moves you. Be it a mountain range, a band of people, the
morning star, or a diesel generator. Breaks through the ego-barrier.
But this touching-deep is as a mirror, and man in his sexual nature

119

has found the clearest mirror to be his human lover. As the West moved into increasing complexities and hierarchies with civilization, Woman as nature, beauty, and The Other came to be an all-dominating symbol; secretly striving through the last three millennia with the Jehovah or Imperator God-figure, a projection of the gathered power of anti-nature social forces. Thus in the Western tradition the Muse and Romantic Love became part of the same energy, and woman as nature the field for experiencing the universe as sacramental. The lovers bed was the sole place to enact the dances and ritual dramas that link primitive people to their geology and the Milky Way. The contemporary decline of the cult of romance is linked to the rise of the sense of the primitive, and the knowledge of the variety of spiritual practices and paths to beauty that cultural anthropology has brought us. We begin to move away now, in this interesting historical spiral, from monogamy and monotheism.

Yet the muse remains a woman. Poetry is voice, and according to Indian tradition, voice, vāk (vox)—is a Goddess. Vāk is also called Sarasvati, she is the lover of Brahma and his actual creative energy; she rides a peacock, wears white, carries a book-scroll and a vīna. The name Sarasvati means "the flowing one." "She is again the Divine in the aspect of wisdom and learning, for she is the Mother of Veda; that is of all knowledge touching Brahman and the universe. She is the Word of which it was born and She is that which is the issue of her great womb, Mahāyoni. Not therefore idly have men worshipped Vāk, or Sarasvati, as the Supreme Power."

As Vāk is wife to Brahma ("wife" means "wave" means "vibrator" in Indo-European etymology) so the voice, in everyone, is a mirror of his own deepest self. The voice rises to answer an inner need; or as BusTon says, "The voice of the Buddha arises, being called forth by the thought of the living beings." In esoteric Buddhism this becomes the basis of a mandala meditation practice: "In their midst is Nayika, the essence of *Ali,* the vowel series—she possesses the true nature of Vajrasattva, and is Queen of the Vajra-realm. She is known as the Lady, as Suchness, as Void, as Perfection of Wisdom, as limit of Reality, as Absence of Self."

The conch shell is an ancient symbol of the sense of hearing, and of the female; the vulva and the fruitful womb. At Koptos there is a bas-relief of a four-point buck, on the statue of the god Min, licking his tongue out toward two conches. There are many Magdalenian bone and horn engravings of bear, bison, and deer licking abstract penises and vulvas. At this point (and from our most archaic past transmitted) the mystery of voice becomes one with the mystery of body.

How does this work among primitive peoples in practice? James Mooney, discussing the Ghost Dance religion, says "There is no limit to the number of these [Ghost Dance] songs, as every trance at every dance produces a new one, the trance subject after regaining consciousness embodying his experience in the spirit world in the form of a song, which is sung at the next dance and succeeding performances until superseded by other songs originating in the same way. Thus a single dance may easily result in twenty or thirty new songs. While songs are thus born and die, certain ones which appeal especially to the Indian heart, on account of their mythology, pathos, or peculiar sweetness, live and are perpetuated."

Modern poets in America, Europe, and Japan, are discovering the breath, the voice, and trance. It is also for some a discovery to realize that the universe is not a dead thing but a continual creation, the song of Sarasvati springing from the trance of Brahma. "Reverence to Her who is eternal, Raudrī, Gaurī, Dhātri, reverence and again reverence, to Her who is the Consciousness in all beings, reverence and again reverence.... Candī says."

Hopscotch and Cats Cradles

> The clouds are "Shining Heaven" with his
> different bird-blankets on
> —Haida

The human race, as it immediately concerns us, has a vertical axis of about 40,000 years and as of 1900 AD a horizontal spread of roughly

3000 different languages and 1000 different cultures. Every living culture and language is the result of countless cross-fertilizations—not a "rise and fall" of civilizations, but more like a flowerlike periodic absorbing—blooming—bursting and scattering of seed. Today we are aware as never before of the plurality of human lifestyles and possibilities, while at the same time being tied, like in an old silent movie, to a runaway locomotive rushing headlong toward a very singular catastrophe. Science, as far as it is capable of looking "on beauty bare" is on our side. Part of our being modern is the very fact of our awareness that we are one with our beginnings—contemporary with all periods—members of all cultures. The seeds of every social structure or custom are in the mind.

The anthropologist Stanley Diamond has said "The sickness of civilization consists in its failure to incorporate (and only then) to move beyond the limits of the primitive." Civilization is so to speak a lack of faith, a human laziness, a willingness to accept the perceptions and decisions of others in place of your own—to be less than a full man. Plus, perhaps, a primate inheritance of excessive socializing; and surviving submission/dominance traits (as can be observed in monkey or baboon bands) closely related to exploitative sexuality. If evolution has any meaning at all we must hope to slowly move away from such biological limitations, just as it is within our power to move away from the self-imposed limitations of small-minded social systems. We all live within skin, ego, society, and species boundaries. Consciousness has boundaries of a different order, "the mind is free." College students trying something different because "they do it in New Guinea" is part of the real work of modern man: to uncover the inner structure and actual boundaries of the mind. The third Mystery. The charts and maps of this realm are called mandalas in Sanskrit. (A poem by the Sixth Dalai Lama runs "Drawing diagrams I measured / Movement of the stars / Though her tender flesh is near / Her mind I cannot measure.") Buddhist and Hindu philosophers have gone deeper into this than almost anyone else but the work is just beginning. We are now gathering all the threads of history together and link-ing modern science to the primitive and archaic sources.

The stability of certain folklore motifs and themes—evidences of linguistic borrowing—the deeper meaning of linguistic drift—the laws by which styles and structures, art-forms and grammars, songs and ways of courting, relate and reflect each other are all mirrors of the self. Even the uses of the word "nature," as in the seventeenth-century witch Isobel Gowdie's testimony about what it was like to make love to the Devil—"I found his nature cold within me as spring-well-water"—throw light on human nature.

Thus nature leads into nature—the wilderness—and the reciprocities and balances by which man lives on earth. Ecology: "eco" (*oikos*) meaning "house" (cf. "ecumnenical"): Housekeeping on Earth. Economics, which is merely the housekeeping of various social orders—taking out more than it puts back—must learn the rules of the greater realm. Ancient and primitive cultures had this knowledge more surely and with almost as much empirical precision (see H. C. Conklin's work on Hanunoo plant-knowledge, for example) as the most concerned biologist today. Inner and outer: the Brihadāranyaka Upanishad says, "Now this Self is the state of being of all contingent beings. In so far as a man pours libations and offers sacrifice, he is in the sphere of the gods; in so far as he recites the Veda he is in the sphere of the seers; in so far as he offers cakes and water to the ancestors, in so far as he gives food and lodging to men, he is of the sphere of men. In so far as he finds grass and water for domestic animals, he is in the sphere of domestic animals; in so far as wild beasts and birds, even down to ants, find something to live on in his house, he is of their sphere."

The primitive world view, far-out scientific knowledge and the poetic imagination are related forces which may help if not to save the world or humanity, at least to save the Redwoods. The goal of Revolution is Transformation. Mystical traditions within the great religions of civilized times have taught a doctrine of Great Effort for the achievement of Transcendence. This must have been their necessary compromise with civilization, which needed for its period to turn man's vision away from nature, to nourish the growth of the social energy. The archaic, the esoteric, and the primitive traditions alike all teach that beyond transcendence is Great Play, and Transformation. After the mind-breaking Void, the emptiness of a million universes appearing and disappearing, all created things rushing into Krishna's devouring mouth; beyond the enlightenment that can say "these beings are dead already; go ahead and kill them, Arjuna" is a loving, simple awareness of the absolute beauty and preciousness of mice and weeds.

Tsong-kha-pa tells us of a transformed universe:

"1. This is a Buddha-realm of infinite beauty
2. All men are divine, are subjects
3. Whatever we use or own are vehicles of worship
4. All acts are authentic, not escapes."

Such authenticity is at the heart of many a primitive world view. For the Anaguta of the Jos plateau, Northern Nigeria, North is called "up"; South is called "down." East is called "morning" and West is called "evening." Hence (according to Dr. Stanley Diamond is his *Anaguta Cosmography*), "Time flows past the permanent central position ... they live at a place called noon, at the center of the world, the only place where space and time intersect." The Australian aborigines live in a world of ongoing recurrence—comradeship with the landscape and continual exchanges of being and form and position; every person, animals, forces, all are related via a web of reincarnation—or rather, they are "interborn." It may well be that rebirth, (or interbirth, for we are actually mutually creating each other and all things while living) is the objective fact of existence which we have not yet brought into conscious knowledge and practice.

It is clear that the empirically observable interconnectedness of nature is but a corner of the vast "jewelled net" which moves from without to within. The spiral (think of nebulae) and spiral conch (vulva/womb) is a symbol of the Great Goddess. It is charming to note that physical properties of spiral conches approximate the Indian notion of the world-creating dance, "expanding form"—"We see that the successive chambers of a spiral Nautilus or of a straight

Orthoceras, each whorl or part of a whorl of a periwinkle or other gastropod, each additional increment of an elephant's trunk, or each new chamber of a spiral foraminifer, has its leading characteristic at once described and its form so far described by the simple statement that it constitutes a *gnomon* to the whole previously existing structure." (D'Arcy Thompson.)

The maze dances, spiral processions, cats cradles, Micronesian string star-charts, mandalas and symbolic journeys of the old wild world are with us still in the universally distributed children's game. Let poetry and Bushmen lead the way in a great hop forward:

"In the following game of long hopscotch, the part marked H is for Heaven: it is played in the usual way except that when you are finishing the first part, on the way up, you throw your tor into Heaven. Then you hop to 11, pick up your tor, jump to the very spot where your tor landed in Heaven, and say, as fast as you can, the alphabet forwards and backwards, your name, address and telephone number (if you have one), your age, and the name of your boyfriend or girlfriend (if you have one of those)" (Patricia Evans, *Hopscotch*).

XII. '67

from
The Real Work (1980)

Craft Interview

The New York Quarterly *"Craft Interview" belongs to an extensive series of interviews about the art of writing conducted by the journal. It was given in 1973 in an office building labyrinth somewhere in Manhattan.*

NYQ: As most of your poems look on the printed page—they're staggered left, right, or indented or something, spaces here and there—are you after visual effect, musical effect, or both?

SNYDER: Well, I consider this very elemental. Most poets I know, most of my colleagues, who follow that open form structuring of the line on the page, do it with full intention as a scoring—as Charles Olson pointed out some years ago in his essay on projective verse.

The placement of the line on the page, the horizontal white spaces and the vertical white spaces are all scoring for how it is to be read and how it is to be timed. Space means time. The marginal indentations are more an indication of voice emphasis, breath emphasis—and, as Pound might have called it, *logopoeia*, some of the dances of the ideas that are working within your syntactic structures.

NYQ: Do you have the poem pretty much complete inside you before you start to put it down to the paper, or is it that you hear this *tala* and that gets you into the poem, but then you are interacting with the paper—or do you use paper—do you use a tape recorder or something?

SNYDER: No, I write by hand when I write. But before I write I do it in my mind many times.

Almost the whole thing. The first step is the rhythmic measure, the second step is a set of preverbal visual images which move to the

rhythmic measure, and the third step is embodying it in words—
and I have learned as a discipline over the years to avoid writing
until I have to. I don't put it on the page until it's ripe—because
otherwise you simply have to revise on the page. So I let it ripen
until it's fully formed and then try to speak the poem out, and as a
rule it falls right into place and completes itself by itself, requiring
only the smallest of minor readjustments and tunings to be just
right to my mind.

NYQ: Do you keep a notebook?

SNYDER: I keep many notebooks—many notebooks and many
useful files.

NYQ: With an idea of these visual images?

SNYDER: Visual, and also working phrases, working images as
written out, even individual words, some of the words that I have
since been working with. This is the way that I am working on
Mountains and Rivers Without End.

NYQ: Do you think of one line of poetry, then, as the melody,
another part as the accompaniment?

SNYDER: Only metaphorically. That leads into another area
which is more structural, structural in regard to imagery over syn-
tax. In that sense metaphorically there are some idea or image lines
that are equivalent to the melody line, and some idea or image
lines which are like a recurrent chorus or a recurrent subtheme, or
repetitions that revolve in various ways, bringing different facets
to light in the unfolding of the poem.

NYQ: Do you rewrite?

SNYDER: No. I tune, I make adjustments, I tamper with it just
a little bit—

NYQ: So that once you have the poem down and you put your
name at the end of it, that's it?

SNYDER: Well, once in a while a poem will come out half-
formed, and what I'll do with that is put it aside totally for several
months and then refer back to it again and then revisualize it all.
I'll replay the whole experience again in my mind. I'll forget all
about what's on the page and get in contact with the preverbal level

behind it, and then by an effort of re-experiencing, recall, visualization, revisualization, I'll live through the whole thing again and try to see it more clearly.

NYQ: Well, this is a kind of information retrieval, almost—you were talking about notebooks and files before, and this is almost an index type of question—Do you keep those in some sort of order, or do you have cross-references?

SNYDER: Yes, they're all organized, but their only function is as mnemonic aids, like signals to open up the inner world. The inner world is too large to ever put down; it's a sea, it's an ocean; and guides and notes and things like that just help me—they're like trail-markers. It's like finding your way back to the beginning of the right path that you were on before, then you can go into it again.

NYQ: Can we talk a minute about the way you go into it—do you use meditation as a way to get into it? Is meditation a way of ...

SNYDER: Curiously, I don't "use" meditation in this way, but it serves me well. I'm a practicing Buddhist, or Buddhist-shamanist, perhaps; and every day I meditate. I do zazen as a daily practice. Which does not mean that my daily meditations are poetic or necessarily profound, but I do them, and in actual fact the inception of the poem generally seems to take its beginnings more while working, rather than while sitting. But the exercise, the practice, of sitting gives me unquestionably an ease of access to the territories of my mind—and a capacity for re-experience—for recalling and revisualizing things with almost living accuracy; and I attribute that to a lot of practice of meditation; although, strictly speaking, that is not the best use of meditation.

NYQ: There's a book around called *Zen in the Art of Archery* by Eugen Herrigel which says that through a kind of disciplined inattention the archer and the target become one. The artist and the creation become one. Do you find that meditation had worked this way for you?

SNYDER: Well, yes, because, like I say, I never try to use meditation deliberately—for the reason that, as anyone who has done much meditation knows, what you aim at is never what you hit.

What you consciously aim at is never what you get. Your conscious mind can't do it for you. So you do have to practice a kind of detached and careful but really relaxed inattention, which lets the unconscious do its own thing of rising and manifesting itself. But the moment you reach out—it's like peripheral vision, almost—the moment you reach out to grab it, it slips back. It's like hunting—it's like still hunting.

Still hunting is when you take a stand in the brush or some place and then become motionless, and then things begin to become alive, and pretty soon you begin to see the squirrels and sparrows and raccoons and rabbits that were there all the time but just, you know, duck out of the way when you look at them too closely. Meditation is like that. You sit down and shut up and don't move, and then the things in your mind begin to come out of their holes and start doing their running around and singing and so forth, and if you just let that happen, you make contact with it.

NYQ: Is that something like what Buddhism calls the *erasure of the self?*

SNYDER: That's one kind of erasure of the self. That's the simplest kind, where the conscious mind temporarily relinquishes its self-importance, its sense of self-importance, of direct focus and decision making and lets peripheral and lower and in some sense deeper aspects of the mind begin to manifest themselves.

What I'm describing I think is common to the creative process for all kinds of people, and all kinds of arts, and they arrive at it not necessarily by formal practice of meditation, but by practice of an intuitive capacity to open the mind and to not cling to too rigid a sense of the conscious self.

NYQ: You have any number of poems—specifically, say, "Shark Meat"—which seem to pull everything together; in fact the very ending of "Shark Meat" speculates that this shark has crisscrossed and has been here before and has now come back to be with us. Is that something like a healing process? Is that what you had in mind in that poem?

SNYDER: In that poem, yes, on not so intense a level. I find it always exciting to me, beautiful, to experience the interdependencies of things, the complex webs and networks by which everything moves, which I think are the most beautiful awarenesses that we can have of ourselves and of our planet. Let me quote something:

> The Buddha once said, bhikshus, if you can understand this blade of rice, you can understand the laws of interdependence and origination. If you can understand the laws of interdependence and origination, you can understand the Dharma. If you understand the Dharma, you know the Buddha.

And again, that's one of the worlds that poetry has taken, is these networks, these laws of interdependence—which are not exactly the laws that science points out. They are—although they are related—but imagination, intuition, vision clarify them, manifest them in certain ways—and to be able to transmit that to others is to transmit a certain quality of truth about the world.

NYQ: There are times when what you've been writing has been what would obviously be called *poetry,* and other times you convey that in what would ordinarily be called *prose*—would you try to explore the border between poetry and prose in your expression, or would you regard those as two separate things?

SNYDER: You are thinking of the essays in *Earth House Hold?*

NYQ: *Earth House Hold* and *The Back Country.* "Why Tribe," for example, is something like that.

SNYDER: Well, *Back Country*, I guess, is really all poetry, to my notion, and *Earth House Hold* is all prose, to my notion. But it's a thin line sometimes. The first difference is that (this is me speaking of my own sense of my own prose) that what I call prose does not have the musical phrase or the rhythm behind it. Nor does it have the content density or the complexity, although the complexity of some of the writing in *Earth House Hold* is fairly—it is fairly complex sometimes. I don't really think of them as different so much as—I adopt whatever structure seems to be necessary to the communication in mind. And I try to keep a clear line between, say, notebook journals, journal jottings and poems—and again, the real line is in the music and the density—although again, to be fair, not all my poems are necessarily that dense in terms of content analysis, but have maybe a musical density sometimes.

What I might add to that is this: I seem to write very different poems. All of the poems that are most interesting to me are different from each other, almost all of them. And I see them almost as different, each one a different form and a different strategy for dealing with a different impulse, and different communication.

There's another level—in the longer loop—we've been talking about short loops now—but in the longer loop I have some concerns that I'm continually investigating that tie together biology, mysticism, prehistory, general systems theory, and my investigations in these things cause me to hit different new centers in interrelationships, different interstices in those networks of ideas and feelings, and when I hit those interstices, sometimes a poem comes out of there, and that's a different place. Each one of them is a different face, many-faceted, of whatever it is I'm trying to work around.

NYQ: The ones you've just described seem to be intellectual, as opposed to emotional concerns.

SNYDER: Yes. Those are emotional-intellectual concerns! Again, they shade off. Like, it's the sanctity or the sacredness of all sentient beings as an emotional concern. The richness and the diversity of all sentient beings and the necessity for the survival of the gene pool for this to continue to be interesting is a biological concern. They shade over into each other.

NYQ: You were talking a couple of minutes ago about activities like logging and pole-skinning—well, you have come to the *NYQ* office by subway. You're giving a poetry reading at the 92nd Street Y tonight. How can you reconcile—how do you manage to put this all together—staying close to what presumably are the sources of your inspiration, like the back country, like these activities, with what a poet has got to do, giving readings and bothering with publishers and being interviewed like this?

SNYDER: Well, I don't find it particularly contradictory, but then contradictions don't bother me. Giving poetry readings is part of my work, because the poem lives in the voice, and I do it not just for the money, although that certainly is a consideration, but because I feel this is where I get to try my poems out and I get to share a little bit of what my sense of the music of them is with others. And I wouldn't feel right if I didn't do that. The poem has to be sung once in a while. To travel around the country is a pleasant luxury, which may not be possible much longer as the whole transportation system will get increasingly expensive and nervous, but as long as it's possible, I'll indulge myself in it and what I gain from that is keeping in touch with the whole amazing network of American intellectual life and seeing many levels of things happening all the time, which I have no objection to seeing, you know. That's part of one's education and keeping one's level of awareness up. Living in the country for me is not a retreat, it's simply placing myself at a different point in the net, a different place in the network, which does not mean that I'm any less interested in the totality of the network, it's simply that's where I center myself.

NYQ: If you lived in the city, do you think you would write very differently from the way you write?

SNYDER: Probably not too differently, especially as I'm learning to see cities as natural objects. I'm getting better able to see what is natural and what is musical.

NYQ: You're stressing finding your own voice, your own identity. Does it help? Has it helped you? Would you recommend that others study with other poets?

SNYDER: Yes. I feel very strongly that poetry also exists as part of a tradition, and is not simply a matter of only private and personal vision, although sometimes something very remarkable comes out of that kind of spontaneous and sort of untutored singing. There are several things that are more universal that we must tap into before personal utterances can become truly poems. One level is the very level of the language and its tradition of songs. We are immediately tied into a tradition by the very fact that we are dealing with

135

the language, and the language is something with an enormous amount of history embedded in it—cultural history.

I feel that one should learn everything about poetry, that he should read everything that he can get his hands on, first from his own tradition and then from every other tradition that he has access to, to know *what* has been done, and to see *how* it has been done. That in a sense is true craft: that one learns by seeing what the techniques of construction were from the past and saves himself the trouble of having to repeat things that others have done that need not be done again. And then also he knows when he writes a poem that has never been written before.

I like to extend it out into other traditions for the very reason that we now are becoming totally cosmopolitan—we might as well do it. For me it's the Chinese tradition and the tradition of Indian vernacular poetry, and also classical Sanskrit poetry of India that I learned most from.

What parallels that is the inner level of universality which is in a sense the collective unconscious that belongs to more than your private self. When you touch on those deeply archetypal things in yourself and at the same time are in touch with what the generations before you have done with the same kind of impulses and the same depths of the mind, then you're able to steer a course with your own voice that will be a new creation, it seems to me. Without that drawing the cross between the personal unconscious to the collective unconscious and one's personal use of language into the collective use of language, you remain simply private. And poetry to be poetry has to speak from a deeper place than the private individual.

NYQ: One thing you've done is translation. *Cold Mountain Poems.* Would you suggest to poets that they get into a fair amount of translating that way?

SNYDER: I'm not sure I would. Translation is too tempting, and I think as an exercise it's good, but it takes you away from yourself finally, from your own work. I think that too many poets take up translating—well, I shouldn't say this. *Some* poets take up translating because they seem to have run out of water in their own well. And maybe they should just keep digging at their own well instead of going over and borrowing it from somebody else's, which is what it seems to be.

Now the way I did the Han-shan translations was very much like what I described earlier. I stumbled on it, you know, that you could read what the Chinese said and then visualize what the Chinese, what the poem was, what the, quote, *"poem"* was, as Robert Duncan would say, the poem that's back there, and see that clear enough to then write down the poem in English directly, then look at the English and check it again against the Chinese and—to make sure that they really weren't too out of line.

NYQ: Do you make it a practice to meet with other poets, poets who have either an affinity for the kind of content, or the kind of resource—like Jerome Rothenberg, for example—do you make it a point to meet with a lot of people that way?

SNYDER: No, I don't make a point of it. One needs a lot of solitude, a lot of silence, to work. I met a lot of poets in the fifties, and we nourished each other in a grand way. We needed each other and we became a small, quote, "culture," warm and moist and nourishing—and we grew out of that, and I—

That was a particularly deep culture of San Francisco for me at that time, and my contact with, first of all, Kenneth Rexroth, my teacher of Chinese poetry Ch'en Shih-hsiang, Philip Whalen, Lew Welch, Michael McClure, Philip Lamantia, Robert Duncan, and other poets of that time—

NYQ: No women?

SNYDER: Not right then. There weren't any that were part of the quote, "culture," that was nourishing itself—not as writers, not that I can recollect. Diane Wakoski a little later, a year or two later. Diane was a very young barefoot girl in San Francisco then, and she began writing, and a little bit later Joanne Kyger came into that, and she's still writing poetry. She and I were married for a while.

But I'm thinking of that initial period. There was indeed a great need for each other, and I have much gratitude for that. *Now,* to the

contrary, I think that poets perhaps place too much importance—
and writers in general—on seeing each other, meeting each other,
talking with each other, going to one person's house, going back to
the other's house, and then saying, "When shall I see you again,"
"Well, let's meet again Wednesday," and then doing it again on
Wednesday and—

Poetry is not a social life. Nor is it a career. It's a vocation. To be
a careerist and to make a social life out of poetry is to waste the best
of your opportunities, probably, for doing your work.

NYQ: You don't teach?

SNYDER: No, I have taught. I taught a year once. And I like to
teach.

NYQ: You did like it?

SNYDER: Oh yes, except you have to talk too much! It's such a
verbal activity, teaching at universities; it depends so much on lan-
guage, just speech. Although it's getting better now. People feel for-
ward enough to have silence in class sometimes, and undertake non-
verbal or only semiverbal ways of teaching sometimes—experiential
ways of teaching. There's something very good that's happening.

NYQ: Do you ever use words purely for the sound, the music,
independent of the meaning of the word?

SNYDER: No. I like to think there is a merger of the sound and
the meaning in some of the poems I have written. I try to steer a
middle path in that.

NYQ: How about rhyme?

SNYDER: I use internal rhyme fairly frequently.

NYQ: Would you say that it just happens?

SNYDER: It just happens, yes.

NYQ: We got a note a few months ago from Charles Bukowski,
who said that craft interviews remind him of people polishing ma-
hogany. Do you have some response to that?

SNYDER: I like to polish mahogany! I like to sharpen my chain
saw. I like to keep all my knives sharp. I like to change oil in the
truck.

Creativity and maintenance go hand in hand. And in a mature